FRESH & WILD

A REAL FOOD ADVENTURE

YSANNE SPEVACK

thorsons

Thorsons
An Imprint of HarperCollins*Publishers*
77–85 Fulham Palace Road,
Hammersmith, London W6 8JB

The website address is: www.thorsonselement.com

and *Thorsons* are trademarks of
HarperCollins*Publishers* Ltd

First published 2004

10 9 8 7 6 5 4 3 2 1

© Ysanne Spevack

Ysanne Spevack asserts the moral right to be
identified as the author of this work

A catalogue record of this book is
available from the British Library

ISBN 0 00 717694 5

Printed and bound in Great Britain by
The Bath Press, Bath

For fresh thinkers and wild spirits

... dedicated to all those who've had enough of
blandness, both in and out of the kitchen, and who
make the world a tastier and better place to
get fresh and be wild.

CONTENTS

PICTURE CREDITS

INTRODUCTION

Anthony Collazos
Customer at Fresh & Wild, Clapham Junction, May 2004.

We are lucky enough to have choices in a world where most are not. Whilst millions of people face starvation every year, we can choose to buy high-calorie, low-nutrition foods from corporations whose ruthlessness beggars belief, or fairly-traded, high-flavour, high-nutrition, artisan-made foods that are as strong on ethics as they are on taste.

If you shop at Fresh & Wild, you have made a choice to support small family farms, wholesome businesses, importers who pay people both locally and in faraway lands fairly, and decent people who believe that craft and artistry are essential to the food we eat. Naturally, you're taste-led too, buying real foods full of flavour for the enjoyment of great eating.

At the end of a hard day's work, the last thing you want to do is make moral and ethical decisions about your shopping. You just want to get a bunch of tasty stuff, go home and eat it. And that's the beauty of Fresh & Wild. Not only is the experience of shopping there so much nicer, but you can trust that their team of buyers have made all the big decisions for you.

You don't have to worry whether the fish is sustainably caught or humanely and safely farmed. There's no need to waste time wondering if the hens that laid the eggs have been routinely injected with antibiotics; if the fruit and veg are covered in pesticides or anti-fungal waxes; if the milk and cheese is full of hormones; or if the breakfast cereals, biscuits and sweets contain dodgy E numbers and battery farm eggs. You can be certain that everything for sale at Fresh & Wild is untainted by all these things, that it's GM-free, full of flavour, full of nutrition and fresh as can be.

It's not really about what it doesn't contain, but what it does. In short, the store is stuffed with real, proper, tasty and unadulterated food – lots of organic foods, lots of imaginative foods, lots of food that you will love. It's not a health food shop so much as a real food shop, full of flavoursome, healthy foods. This can be a bit of a culture shock if you're used to the standard run-of-the-mill supermarket sweep.

That's where this book comes in. I want you to explore, experiment and have lots of fun with things that you've never tried before. Fresh & Wild has plenty of staple foods that you know exactly how to eat – like the excellent hand-baked organic breads, or incredible artisan cheeses, or the many varieties of apples, cucumbers and potatoes – but what exactly is mochi? And what are you supposed to do with burdock roots, nori, or Ras-el-Hanout?

I love playing with food. Mixing and matching the most amazing ingredients and recipes from near and far, sometimes making an authentic meal from another continent, other times cooking up a mélange that could only happen in a multicultural city like London or Bristol. We're blessed with choices, so why not enjoy the amazing opportunities we have to tickle our taste buds with local, traditional delicacies or exotic, fairly-traded delights? And have a browse at the culinary gadgets they've got, too. The Rookie chopsticks are great for kids, while the cast-iron griddle pans are top for char-grilling just about anything, from fennel to fish.

Ingredients listed in this book are mostly available in season at Fresh & Wild. The stores vary from location to location, as each local Fresh &

Wild has its own customers with different preferences, so the managers tailor their products accordingly. So Clapham's got lots of organic baby food and family favourites, while Soho's geared up for single creatives in their twenties. And Notting Hill satisfies the needs of lots of local models and pop stars, so that's the one for Dr Haushka cosmetics and luxurious delicacies.

The food on offer at all Fresh & Wild stores develops and changes to reflect what you, the customer, want. Some ingredients prove majorly popular and spread throughout the network of stores like wildfire. Others are popular at just a couple of locations whilst customers at the other shops don't go for them. So in short, if your Fresh & Wild doesn't seem to have one of the ingredients you need to make a particular recipe, let them know that your community wants it stocked.

Of course, some really unusual ingredients can't be guaranteed to be on the shelves 365 days every year. The availability of seasonal and niche foods comes and goes, so plan ahead if you want to try some of the recipes with stranger and more exotic things in them. For instance, fresh wood blewit mushrooms aren't seasonal, as they're farmed in Sussex, but they're unlikely to be stocked all the time, in all the Fresh & Wild stores, until enough people like you and I buy them regularly enough to make it worth their while.

So let's make it happen by buying strange ingredients. Let's keep small artisan food crafts alive. Let's make sure that those special little ingredients stick around for future generations to enjoy. Oh yes, let's have some fun in the kitchen.

All recipes in this book are for organic, fresh produce: organic meat, organic poultry, organic milk, organic soy products and organic eggs – and luckily they're the only kind on offer at Fresh & Wild. Where a recipe includes eggs these are large hen eggs unless it says otherwise. All fish recipes are for organically-farmed fish or sustainably-caught wild fish. Some of the cheeses mentioned are organic, a few are not, but all are proper artisan-produced, slow food delicacies. All oils are cold pressed, the honey isn't heat-treated and there are no artificial chemical preservatives, colourings or flavourings to be found in any ingredients listed.

Use any of the different kinds of salt in the stores, as they're all from clean waters and have no strange things added like the sodium hexaflourocyanate generally found in salt. I particularly like Malden and Geo Atlantic, but try them all and be amazed at their subtly different flavours. And all butter listed in the ingredients is unsalted unless it says it's salted.

I've confidently used things like lemon zest in the recipes, as organic citrus fruit don't include loads of wax and pesticides and are therefore ready to zest. Some of the fresh vegetables, like rainbow chard and burdock root, are only available as organic produce. It makes sense that if you're a farmer growing a very special or heirloom variety, you're the kind of person that wants to go the whole hog and grow it the best way. Lots of the spices are only available organic too, although some are only available uncertified for now.

I'm only happy to write recipes that taste delicious *and* feel good for the people who grew the ingredients, whether they're in faraway countries or on our own doorstep. Ingredients grown in the tropics and sold at Fresh & Wild are always fairly traded, like dried papaya and cassia bark. When you buy British organic ingredients at Fresh & Wild, like carrots and lamb, you can be confident that our farmers are paid fairly for their hard work and early January mornings, something that's rarely the case in many other stores.

Next time you venture into a shop that's not Fresh & Wild, please read the small print on their wares. Take a closer look at the eco-sensitivity of the packaging on those organic bananas. Read about the sustainability of the fish in that gas-filled pack. Check out those long words on the side of the biscuits, next to the listing for liquid eggs that they don't point out come from inhumane battery farms. I can't help but see the tarnish, the corner cutting, the injustice to farmers, the potential for health and morals to be undermined.

That's why I run back to decent food, happy to part with a few extra pence for apples that aren't unripe Golden Delicious; apples without a covering of anti-fungal waxes and without a cocktail of pesticides on their skin – apples that are full of nutrients, properly ripened and bursting with flavour ...

Happy eating!

Ysanne x

PS Let me know how you're enjoying these recipes by emailing hello@organicfood.co.uk. If I'm busy, someone else will read your email, but rest assured that I'll get to hear what you have to say. Have fun!

BREAKFAST

Chris Walford
Pertwood Organic Cereals, Hindon, Wiltshire

'Given my previous anxieties about food security and quality, and my love of real food, it is a privilege to be part of something which is rooted in traditional artisan skills and sustainable practices.'

Breakfast really is the most important meal of the day.

Scientific studies have found that breakfast-eaters apparently have fewer accidents, achieve higher levels of success in work and better exam results, earn more money and generally enjoy better health than those who skip breakfast.

But day after day, week after week, even those who make sure they eat this wonder-meal rely on exactly the same food each morning. Too groggy to start getting fancy in the kitchen, we shovel the same tried and tested formula into our mouths and run out the door. No other meal gets this little attention. If you had the very same sandwich every day for lunch, you'd soon get bored. So why put up with the same old breakfast?

The key to sorting out this sorry state of affairs is planning. Don't leave it to the morning rush to make decisions about what grub to munch. Make a decision the night before and get the things you need together. Better still, some breakfast recipes can to be cooked up in batches and frozen, so you only need to plan them now and then – so long as you remember to take them out the freezer the night before.

Start your day with a twist of lemon juice in a mug of warm water. You're welcome to go for a cup of tea or coffee after that, but try the lemon water for a week and you'll be hooked. The warm, diluted juice wakes up your kidneys and liver, ready to cleanse your blood for the rest of the day – which means better skin, better digestion and a clearer head. Just what the doctor ordered.

And get a bunch of proper measuring spoons. The spoons in your kitchen drawer are almost certainly different measures from the standard 5ml for a teaspoon or 15ml for a tablespoon used in recipes. If you want to get accurate results, measuring spoons are great and they'll cost you less than a fiver.

BUCKWHEAT BLINTZES

with Creamy Blackberry and Barley Malt Sauce

Despite its name, buckwheat has nothing to do with wheat, but is a gluten-free grain that was originally from the icy wastelands of Siberia. Popular in Eastern Europe, the flour can be successfully used in cakes, puddings and pastries. It has a stronger, nuttier, earthier flavour than wheat, making it a lovely partner to this sweet malt syrup topping.

True blintzes are always made out of buckwheat flour, as they originally come from Russia. They're thicker than Pancake Day pancakes and much smaller in diameter. They're also chewier and tastier. A cross between pancakes and crumpets, blintzes are the dumplings of the pancake world.

Blackberries are delicious and powerfully good for you, as they're full of vitamin C and antioxidants. They've also got lots of vitamin E in them, courtesy of the little blackberry seeds. Organic blackberries have the added benefit of not having been sprayed with pesticides – unlike non-organic soft fruit, which is usually covered in the stuff. And it's generally agreed that organic summer berries like these taste a lot more intense, and are sweeter too, than their non-organic counterparts.

There are loads of wild blackberries in some areas of the UK, so if there seem to be tons in your area this autumn, just waiting to be picked, then get picking. Watch out for the prickles and make sure that you only pick those growing away from roads, so they're not high in pollutants from car fumes. And don't pick them in an area specifically high in special wild birds, as they'll want to eat them, too. Soak the freshly picked blackberries in a deep bowl of salt water for an hour or so, by which time any grubs and bugs will have risen to the surface, then rinse the berries well in fresh water.

If blackberries are out of season when you make these blintzes, use a preserved summer fruit, like Biona's blueberries in a jar.

They're stored in syrup, so simply squash the entire contents of the jar into the yogurt, but skip the malt syrup and lemon so that the sauce isn't too sweet.

This is a breakfast treat to give you zing all day long.

BUCKWHEAT BLINTZES

with Creamy Blackberry and Barley Malt Sauce

TO SERVE 5 PEOPLE WITH 2 PANCAKES EACH:

100g buckwheat flour
¼ of a nutmeg, grated
½ teaspoon ground cinnamon
1 teaspoon baking powder
1 egg
150ml semi-skimmed or soy milk
2 tablespoons sunflower oil

FOR THE SAUCE:
100g punnet of blackberries, squashed with a fork
250g goat's yogurt
Juice of ½ a lemon
2 tablespoons barley malt syrup

Mix the flour, spices and baking powder in a big mixing bowl, then make a hollow in the middle. With a wooden spoon, mix in the egg and then the milk, slowly and a bit at a time, to make a thick batter.

Put the squashed berries in separate bowl and add the yogurt, lemon juice and malt syrup, mixing well to make a sauce. Leave it to one side so the juices can mingle.

Heat half the oil in a frying pan, then drop the batter in, one rounded tablespoon at a time for each blintz. Spread the blob out a bit with the back of the metal spoon so that each blintz is about 6–7cm wide. Add the rest of the oil after you've fried about half the blintzes. Fry for 1–2 minutes until brown, then turn each one over to cook the other side for a few more minutes.

Serve immediately, drizzled in the blackberry sauce.

PARSEE PARSLEY POTATOES 'N' EGGS

Let's widen the palette of flavours that your breakfast can include. Why not add some chilli and fragrant spices to kick-start your day this morning? In many countries all over the world, people get busy with strong flavours first thing. On a visit to New Mexico, I was regularly asked by waitresses in breakfast diners 'do you want that with red, green or Christmas?' – meaning, red chilli salsa, green chilli salsa, or both. Wakey, wakey!

The inspiration for this poached egg recipe is an ancient Parsee recipe taught to me by Cyrus Todiwala, an extraordinary chef who founded the Asian and Oriental School of Cookery in Hoxton, London. The school teaches disadvantaged local kids how to cook traditional recipes and then places them into good culinary jobs (deservedly Cyrus received an MBE in recognition of the skill he has in motivating and inspiring the students to flourish).

I've expanded the original recipe to include celeriac and kohlrabi, because I like them, plus I've added some different spices and European flavours like olive oil and parsley. It's a mix between a Parsee dish and a French dauphinoise dish, but quicker, lighter and made on the hob instead of in the oven. I love it, especially the morning after the night before.

PARSEE PARSLEY POTATOES 'N' EGGS

BREAKFAST FOR 4 NORMAL PEOPLE, OR 2 GREEDY ONES:

3 tablespoons olive oil

¼ teaspoon cumin seeds, pounded with a pestle

¼ teaspoon fenugreek seeds, pounded with a pestle

¼ teaspoon mustard seeds, pounded with a pestle

2 garlic cloves, peeled and crushed

1 fresh green chilli, seeds and membrane removed, and crushed

1 medium onion, peeled and thinly sliced

1 small potato, scrubbed and thinly sliced

1 small kohlrabi, washed and thinly sliced

⅓ celeriac, scrubbed and thinly sliced

A pinch of salt

4 eggs, 1 of which is washed thoroughly and dried

A handful of fresh parsley, finely chopped

Heat the oil in a large, deep frying pan, over a medium heat, and add the pounded spice seeds when it's hot. Sauté for a minute, stirring with a wooden spatula, and then add the garlic and chilli. Stir this about for another minute, then add the onion and keep frying for a few minutes until it's going opaque. Add the potato, kohlrabi and celeriac, fry for a few minutes and then pour in enough water to nearly cover the vegetables. Throw in a pinch of salt, cover the pan, lower the heat, and leave to slowly simmer for about 10 minutes.

Check if the vegetables are cooked; if not, leave it to simmer for a couple more minutes. When they're tender, sprinkle in the parsley and turn the mixture slowly with the spatula, taking care not to break the vegetables up too much. Level the vegetables out again, then take the clean egg and use the outside of the shell to make four dips in the mixture at regularly spaced intervals. Crack all of the eggs, putting one into each dip.

Put the lid back on the pan and slowly cook over a low heat until the egg yolks are poached to your liking. Cut into quarters with the edge of a fish slice and serve up with crusty bread and butter.

GRANOLA

Everybody in America knows about this stuff, but it's not often made in the UK. I don't know why – it's so quick and easy, perfumes your kitchen with a sweet home-baking smell, is deliciously good for you and saves a fortune on decent muesli. Before preparing the granola, make sure you have a big re-usable plastic container to store it in.

Granola can be served with any kind of milk. All organic cow's milk is good quality milk, scientifically proven to contain at least 60 per cent more alpha-linoleic acids (which help to keep your heart healthy) than non-organic milk. I make a point of buying Manor Farm milk. Pam and Will Best, the couple whose cows produce it, have been dedicated dairy farmers for over 35 years and their experience and care is reflected not only in the texture and creaminess of the milk but in its sweet, clean taste.

Part of the reason Manor Farm's milk tastes so sweet is that the cows munch on clover, chicory, alfalfa and other sweet-tasting salad crops. These are planted for practical cow-welfare and soil-enriching reasons, but they also add a back note to the final pint. Or maybe their cows are just particularly content. However, the main difference between Manor Farm's milk and almost every other organic cow's milk is that it's not been homogenized.

Homogenization is a mechanical process that became widespread with the demise of the milkman and the rise of the supermarket. When we were kids, we shook a recyclable glass milk bottle every morning before pouring the milk. Or, if we were feeling naughty, we'd have the top of the milk when our mums weren't looking. When everyone started buying milk in those plastic bottle-like containers that now inhabit every fridge door, the marketing men decided that the cream floating on top of our pints was an unsightly blemish. Something had to be done, and that something was homogenization.

The milk is squeezed through a tiny tube at very high pressure, so that all the lovely cream globules break down into tiny-weeny cream globules that you don't notice and therefore can't enjoy. All the unsightly cream disappears and the plastic bottle-like containers look fat-free. Of course they're not really any lower in fat, plus they take away the freedom of choice to either go for the cream or avoid it.

There are no chemicals involved with homogenization, so it's perfectly legal for organic milk producers to do it. It just doesn't seem like the greatest idea to me – processing purely for cosmetic reasons. And there's some evidence building that homogenized milk is bad for your heart.

I don't know about that, but what I do know is that non-homogenized milk tastes better, has a better texture and allows the drinker to choose top-of-the-milk or shaken-up. And it comes in a paper-based carton, as opposed to a plastic bottle that will never decompose.

But back to breakfast, a time of happy optimism. When they're in season, you can use cobnuts instead of hazelnuts in recipes, as cobnuts are simply a local Kentish type of hazelnut. They're officially in season from St Philbert's day on 23rd August until Christmas Day. Cobnuts are always sold as a whole nut and generally wrapped in their individual green leafy coats. They're long and thumbnail-shaped, succulent and delicious, with a milder flavour than the round hazelnuts you get pre-shelled in packets. Make sure you do the shelling when nobody's about, otherwise all the nuts are guaranteed to be gobbled up before the granola hits the oven.

Popped amaranth also features in this granola mix. This tiny seed from South America is a very special grain that's like no other.

I went on a solo journey into the Amazon some years ago and found it a very hot, scary and noisy experience, with hundreds of animals and insects making a major racket all night long with their scuttling around, buzzing and general liveliness. Anyway, the local people paint their faces with an orangey-red natural greasepaint, which looks wicked and protects their skin from the sun, as it's a bonafide total sun block. This stuff is made out of amaranth flower heads, which are big fluffy, feathery things.

Inside the flowers are thousands of tiny amaranth seeds, about 50,000 seeds per plant. The seeds are highly nutritious, full of protein and fibre, and also rich in iron, calcium and vitamin A. In fact, they contain double the amount of calcium as cow's milk and five times more iron than wheat. And they're also one of the only types of seed that can be popped, just like popcorn, as opposed to the many that are actually puffed, like rice.

So why aren't we all eating lots of lovely amaranth? It's all down to history. The Spanish conquistadors banned amaranth from polite society after discovering the traditional Aztec ritual use of these little seeds. Aztec women made sacred little dollies out of ground amaranth seeds, honey and their own monthly blood, for ceremonial eating, emulating human sacrificial rites. Quite frankly, this didn't go down at all well with the 16th-century Spanish colonialists, who nearly wiped out the grain from the face of the earth, such was their shock and outrage.

Luckily, a few remote communities deep in the Andes kept amaranth in existence, probably because it forms the basis of the local homebrew of Peru, a highly alcoholic and, in my experience, quite revolting beverage called *chicha* that seems to keep the local lads and ladettes of Lima laughing.

The Aztec dolly cakes do live on in Mexico, where they've evolved to become the popped amaranth and sugar cake *alegria*, which means 'happiness'. A nice thought for the day.

GRANOLA

500g rolled oats (i.e. small porridge oats)

50g walnut pieces

50g chopped hazelnuts or 50g chopped cobnuts

50g sunflower seeds

50g pumpkin seeds

50g sesame seeds

100g juicy dried sultanas

8 tablespoons safflower oil

4 tablespoons brown rice malt syrup

3 tablespoons date syrup

50g popped amaranth

Preheat the oven to 180°C/350°F/Gas Mark 4. In a big bowl, mix all the dry ingredients thoroughly. In a small frying pan, gently heat the oil and syrups to combine them. Stir this mixture into the dried ingredients as soon as syrup goes runny. Divide the granola between two baking trays, spreading it out so that it's no more than 3cm deep. Put it in the hot oven and stir it with a wooden spoon every 10 minutes.

It should be ready in about 20 minutes. Check it and remove the trays when the oats have just gone golden rather than waiting until they go brown. Once it's out the oven, immediately stir in the popped amaranth so it sticks to the hot syrupy clumps.

Leave to cool before eating. Save the rest in a container.

Try homemade granola with nut milks like hazelnut or almond milk, and get a doubly nut whammy. You can buy-ready made nut milks at Fresh & Wild, but to make your own, simply soak about 50g ground nuts (as in nuts that have been ground, not American peanuts) in about 100ml boiling water for quarter of an hour. Strain the milky liquid, throw away the solids and try adding a touch of malt.

HOT RICE CONGEE

This Chinese recipe is the first meal of the day for most of the planet's population. If you generally have cereal and milk, you might find it a bit heavy. However, if you prefer your breakfast savoury, give it a go and see just why it's so popular around the globe. I recommend cooking up a batch over the weekend ready to simply reheat on weekday mornings.

TO MAKE 3 PORTIONS YOU'LL NEED:

100g white long grain rice
400g Joubere (or 400ml homemade) vegetable or chicken stock
1 tablespoon chopped takuan (pickled daikon root)
3cm piece fresh ginger root, grated
1 heaped teaspoon dried organic mandarin peel, soaked in water

SPRINKLE ON TOP:
Chopped spring onion
Chopped fresh coriander
Chopped sushi ginger

Combine all of the congee ingredients in a saucepan and bring to the boil. Turn down the heat so that the mixture simmers slowly. Simmer for about an hour, checking now and then if you need to add more liquid. Cook the congee until it has the consistency of porridge or thick soup. Sprinkle over the topping to taste and tuck in.

For a nuttier consistency, use brown basmati rice instead of, or in combination with, the white rice. Use about 300g of Joubere (or 300ml of homemade) stock to 100g of brown rice. All liquid volumes are flexible depending on how gooey you like it.

APPLE PORRIDGE

There's dried fruit and there's dried fruit, and Fresh & Wild is home to some pretty awesome dried fruit. We're talking intense flavours, enticing varieties, bright colours – and it's fairly traded by people who care about mutually beneficial interaction. That means we get the very best quality commodity, produced lovingly to the best of a community's abilities, and the growers get the respect they deserve and a fair price to reflect their hard work and value. This is the kind of trade that makes the world a better place.

This recipe has a standard oat porridge base, but is creamier because it's soaked. It's flavoured with a deliciously vibrant mix of apples and tropical fruit, all spiced to wake you up with a zing.

The crushed nuts **add an interesting texture** and a good mix of oils and proteins.

All in all, this porridge is good for you, tastes divine and improves somebody else's day in a faraway country.

APPLE PORRIDGE

FOR 4 BOWLS OF STEAMING HOT PORRIDGE:

3 moist prunes, pitted

2 juicy Crazy Jack's soft-dried figs

3 Tropical Wholefoods sliced dried star fruit

2 Southern Alps dried strawberries from their slow-dried fruit mix

50g walnut pieces

30g almonds

1 teaspoon ground cinnamon

4 whole cloves

250ml proper pressed apple juice

200g porridge oats

400ml good quality soy milk, such as Bonsoy

1 small fresh eating apple, such as a Cox

The night before, chop all the dried fruit except the strawberries. These are too brittle to chop, so should be quartered with kitchen scissors or left whole if you don't have a pair. Put the nuts in a plastic bag, squeeze the air out and bash them with a rolling pin. Put the prepared dried fruit and nuts into a bowl with the spices, and cover with the apple juice. Put the oats and soy milk in a saucepan and leave to soak.

Next morning, heat the saucepan over a low heat, topping up with more soy milk if it's not looking runny enough for you. Stir the porridge frequently with a wooden spoon. Pick the cloves out of the soaked fruit.

Finely grate the fresh apple and mix it into the fruit mixture. Keep heating the porridge, letting it come to the boil. Let it bubble for a minute or so, stirring all the time, then take it off the heat and add the fruit mixture.

Stir this in, then divide the porridge between four serving bowls. Put bottles of maple, agave and date syrups on the table for people to help themselves.

GAMUT OF KAMUT®

Go Egyptian this morning with a bowl of Nefertiti's favourite grain (well, probably). The name 'kamut' comes from the ancient Egyptian word for wheat, and this grain is a predecessor of modern durum wheat. Kamut, however, is a third richer in protein, has loads of minerals and vitamins and a lovely buttery flavour.

Even though the two grains are closely related, studies and individual experience have proven that kamut can be enjoyed by many gluten-sensitive people with no adverse reactions. Of course, people diagnosed with coeliac disease should consult their doctor before experimenting with this grain, but if you want to add more variety to your diet, it's a great grain to have up your sleeve.

Barley is another under-used grain, with a fairly strong flavour and excellent nutritional profile. Barley semolina is a very soothing kind of food, with its comforting texture and high quantity of B vitamins – the vitamin group that's particularly good at helping the body cope with stress. Barley is also medicinally soothing for your intestines as it travels around the tubes, plus it gently relieves inflammations like cystitis or constipation, making it the perfect gentle accompaniment to kamut first thing in the morning.

Agave syrup is made from agave plants, one of a family of succulents that provide the starter for making tequila.

Deep in the Mexican desert, the agave plant was revered by Aztecs of old as the Tree of Life and Plenty, and its juice was used in their sacred rites. Nowadays, it's a welcome addition to your breakfast. It's sweeter to the taste than refined sugar, but is a valuable complex food with no mono-saccharides. In plain speak this means you don't get the roller coaster effect of a sugar high followed by a sugar crash when you sweeten with agave syrup.

For this breakfast recipe, it's best to boil up your kamut grain the night before to save having to wait for your breakfast. Even better, boil a batch at the weekend and freeze it in individual portions ready to use through-out the week. Simply leave a frozen portion of kamut out the night before for de-frosted, cooked grain the next morning.

GAMUT OF KAMUT®

BREAKFAST FOR 4 HUNGRY PEOPLE:

50g dried hunza apricots
150g kamut® grain
100g barley semolina
1 teaspoon ground cinnamon
¼ teaspoon ground mace or nutmeg
1 vanilla pod
600ml soy milk
Agave syrup to taste

The night before you want this breakfast, soak the dried hunza apricots in 100ml of lukewarm water. Simmer the kamut grain in 500ml of water for about an hour and a half, checking every half hour or so that the saucepan hasn't boiled dry. If it does, simply add some more water and simmer until the grain is cooked. It will be firm and chewy in texture when it's done.

In the morning, mix the cooked kamut, the uncooked semolina, the spices, the vanilla and the apricot soaking liquor in a large saucepan. Add the soy milk and bring to the boil over a high heat. Turn the heat right down so that the liquid is just simmering, and keep simmering with the lid on for about 6–7 minutes. Add the whole apricots and stir them in, then keep cooking and stirring with a wooden spoon until the semolina is done. This will be about another 10 minutes or so.

When it's ready, spoon it into individual bowls. Put the syrup on the table so everyone can sweeten the Gamut of Kamut to suit their tastes.

J O'S **PORAGE**

Jo is a newspaper pictures editor turned silversmith, who lives near Canary Wharf in London's East End. She swears by this breakfast idea and is full of creativity and beans, so give it a go.

Millet is a wonder grain. It's one of the richest sources of silicon, the mineral that's a major ingredient in collagen. Collagen is not just something that's used in cosmetic surgery. It's the substance that keeps everything in your body flexible – your skin, your eyes and your arteries. Millet is also the only grain to contain all eight of the essential amino acids needed for a complete protein. This breakfast is nice and alkaline, too, as millet is also the only grain that is alkaline, so it's a real treat for your liver. Full of complex carbohydrates, it will keep you alert and on the ball until lunchtime, with the rice, nuts and fruit providing the starches.

Actually, most of southern Africa swears by millet, whether flaked, whole or ground into flour. It's the staple food grown by farmers in and around Zimbabwe, where it grows well even in near-drought conditions. People used to rely on maize in Zimbabwe, in the same way that people in the UK rely on wheat. But maize needs regular watering, leaving subsistence farmers in southern Africa without a crop if the rains don't come.

Millet is beginning to turn this around, as it's one of the hardiest food crops you can grow. Being a native African grain, it can survive long periods of drought and short periods of flood. So it's bringing hope of self-sufficiency in the future to the farmers and communities who live in this area. And as it's a much richer food source than maize, it adds valuable protein and nutrition to their diets.

JO'S **PORAGE**

TO MAKE 2 PORTIONS:

4 heaped tablespoons millet flakes
4 heaped tablespoons brown rice flakes
2 heaped tablespoons sultanas
1 heaped tablespoon flaked almonds
500ml oat milk

Put all the dry ingredients into a saucepan and add enough cold water to cover. Leave this overnight with the lid on. In the morning, add the oat milk and warm over a low heat. For an alternative, try adding a teaspoon of ground cinnamon to the dry mixture and soaking it in apple juice.

SAVOURY SCRAMBLED TOFU

Scrambled eggs are lovely first thing in the morning, but why not try scrambled tofu for a change? As with perfect egg scrambling, perfect tofu scrambling is all down to a slow, gentle cook.

Fresh & Wild stock a good range of tofus from different British tofu makers, many of which are hand-crafted by skilled artisans. Give it a go and you'll be smiling all day.

SAVOURY SCRAMBLED TOFU

SERVES 4 PEOPLE:

2 tablespoons tahini

2 tablespoons shoyu

500g piece of firm tofu

1 tablespoon hemp oil or sunflower oil

1 tablespoon toasted sesame oil

2 big Portabella mushrooms or 4 chestnut mushrooms, sliced

2 tomatoes, chopped

1 large spring onion, trimmed and finely chopped

Black pepper, gomasio and green nori flakes to taste

Mix the tahini and shoyu in a bowl to form a gloopy paste. Crumble the tofu into the tahini bowl, stirring the mixture to cover the tofu with the paste. Heat the oils in a medium-sized frying pan over a low heat. Add the mushrooms to the pan once the oil is hot enough to make them gently sizzle. Fry the mushrooms, moving them about with a wooden spoon.

After 3–4 minutes, add the tomatoes and spring onions. Keep stirring to make sure the veg doesn't stick. Add the tofu to the pan and gently cook until everything is piping hot and smells good. Serve with fresh crusty bread and butter, and put the pepper, gomasio or nori flakes on the table so everyone can season their own breakfast to individual perfection.

LUNCH

Suzanne Cook
Dorset Hams, Beaminster, Dorset

'It might sound like a cliché, but quality, not quantity is really the name of the game here at Dorset Hams. We operate from under one roof, where we can control everything. We do things our way, on a small scale, and that's the way we like it.'

If you're reading this book, you're probably a regular lunch eater at your local Fresh & Wild. But what if you're a full-time mum, freelance, retired person, student or loafer?

And how about the weekend and days off?

You could rustle up a boring sandwich if you want ... or try these delicious and nutritious alternatives.

Happy lunch munching!

SQUID AND SALCHICHÓN
with Dulse

Big squids, ready to have their tentacles removed and cooked. Their handy ink sacs hidden inside their strange blobby bodies, waiting to be pierced and the black liquid dripped into homemade pasta mixes. These guys really are the B-movie stars of the fish counter.

Of course, the A-list fish counter celebs have to be the guys that know how to prepare the fish and seafood ready for your dinner. It takes years of practice and innate flair to be able to de-tube, de-tentacle and clean up squids. So I'm not going to attempt a 'here's how you do it' paragraph – simply ask your friendly Fresh & Wild fishmonger to sort it out for you, then get it home and into the pan.

If your local store is the Notting Hill shop, chances are the tentacle chopper extraordinaire will be Jeff Rotheram. He's totally committed to widening your enjoyment of fish and he'll happily guide you through the more unusual guys on the ice between you and him. Jeff has been a fishmonger for over 25 years and can tell you where the fish on his counter are from, why he likes them and practically what their mothers were called. Before arriving at Fresh & Wild, Jeff worked at Harvey Nichols and before that at a fantastic Cornish fish wholesaler, so he can help you out with your dinner choices, no problem.

Unlike squid, salchichón is easy – just get it out of the packet or ask the deli counter lady to cut you some. Et voilà. Salchichón is a very traditional cured sausage, originally from the town of Cantimpalos in Segovia, but with regional variations now from every part of Spain. It's a bit like chorizo, which also comes from this town, but is thinner and longer, with more garlic and less paprika, and is dried into a U shape. Catalan salchichón has black pepper in it, while salchichón from the town of Vic in the Pyrenees is thicker than most, at about 5cm instead of 3–4cm.

As with most cured salamis and saucissons, a lot of pork fat goes into this dried sausage along with the pork, so go easy on the butter for this recipe.

You only need a tiny bit of butter to get the sausage started. After that, its own fat will melt and provide enough to fry itself and the squid.

Talking of pork fat, don't forget that all mammals store the more toxic elements from their bodies in their fat. If you want to eat piggy fat from animals that have been raised in concrete sties without any windows – animals that wade about knee deep in pig poo, attacking each other and constantly getting diseases – then go for it. Personally, I'd stick to eating organic pigs, who are raised with access to fresh air and sunlight, and enjoy a lot more freedom to roam, less crowded quarters to live in, and are only given veterinary drugs if they get sick, rather than as a preventative measure. And that means using organic salchichón in this lovely lunch dish.

The dulse for this recipe comes fresh from seas off the coast of France. It plays a delicate supporting role to the Cornish squid and is a really great local sea vegetable that's as mineral-rich as some dried Japanese sea veg.

All in all, this is an extremely quick lunch dish that's full of the freshest sea flavours, plus a special bit of extra meaty spice.

SQUID AND SALCHICHÓN
with Dulse

LUNCH FOR 2:

1 teaspoon butter
100g salchichón slices, snipped with scissors into little pieces
200g prepared squid, chopped into bite-sized chunks
A punnet of fresh dulse, washed and finely chopped or a handful
  of dried dulse, soaked for 10 minutes and then drained
White wine vinegar to taste
Pepper to taste

Melt the butter in a medium frying pan over a high heat. When it's hot, throw in the salchichón and fry for about a minute, stirring with a wooden spatula. Then chuck in the squid and the dulse and fry together for about 3 minutes more, coating in the fat from the sausage.

Take the pan off the heat and dish up with some really good bread. Put the vinegar and pepper on the table for you and your co-eater to help yourselves. Treat yourselves to some white wine as an accompaniment.

TOMORROW'S **TAMALES**

Tamales (pronounced *tam-aaah-lees*) are the sandwiches of South America. They consist of a flavoursome filling that is encased in a starchy dough and then cooked inside a husk of corn. Traditionally, special maize flour called masa harina (literally 'dough flour') is used to make the masa (dough). However, for this recipe, I've used polenta, simply because you can't get masa harina in the UK – especially not organic masa harina. May this sorry state of affairs change soon. Until it does, polenta is a really good substitute.

Polenta is a maize-based floury substance from Italy that's usually used to make a thick, savoury porridge. But it also makes a tasty, light dough for tamales when you cook it with half the usual amount of liquid. You can try flavouring the dough with chilli or dried herbs, or try adding other non-authentic flavourings like dried mushrooms, pesto or anchovy paste. You could also use the dough to make Corn Pones – simply bake the dough in muffin trays.

I've called this recipe Tomorrow's Tamales because they can be prepared the night before, ready to be steamed for lunch the next day. But once the tamales have been steamed, eat them up there and then because The-Day-After-Tomorrow's Tamales will have lost their squidge and turned into dry rock cakes.

Fresh as daisies, these guys are succulent, filling and generally fabamundo.

TOMORROW'S **TAMALES**

FOR THE DOUGH:

200g polenta

300g Joubere (or 300ml homemade) chicken stock

A big knob of butter

1½ teaspoons baking powder

Heat all the dough ingredients in a pan over a medium heat. Using an open whisk, beat the mixture well as it cooks. This action will keep the dough light and fluffy. When cooked through, take the dough off the heat and leave it to cool.

FOR THE FILLING:

You can fill tamales with just about anything, even sweet fillings. Try soaking dried mushrooms or tomatoes, then chopping them to make a stuffing. Sauté some fresh spinach by steaming it in its own water. Simply wash the spinach, then put the wet leaves into a frying pan over a medium heat and it will steam within a few minutes. Use some fried shrimps or flaky fish like cod or lemon sole, or fry up some shredded chicken or pork. You could also use up some of last night's dinner leftovers, or try some of the ready-made meze ingredients available in store, such as:

Roasted artichoke hearts

Roasted onions

Grilled aubergines
Pomorella – sun-dried tomato paste
Asparagus cream
Roasted red peppers

FOR THE WRAPPING:
Some outer leaves from fresh sweetcorn ears, or baking paper

If you're using fresh sweetcorn leaves, they'll be pliable enough to use as a wrapping. I've got into the habit of keeping all my sweetcorn leaves, so that when corn is not in season, I can still make tomorrow's tamales. If you're using dried leaves, soak them in warm water overnight, so they become fully flexible again. If you want, use baking paper instead, as it's just as good in terms of keeping the tamales at the right moisture level. However, leaf-wrapped tamales look nice and appetizing, and this is how they're always served in South and Central American countries.

Once you've chosen your flavouring *du jour*, take two-thirds of the dough out of the pan, divide it into six equal bits and shape these into 7–8cm × 2–3cm rectangles. Make a little channel along each one and fill it with the filling of your choice. Divide the remaining dough into six, shape into lids and use to cover the filled rectangles. Make sure the filling is totally hidden and that the lids are squashed together with the bottoms so that they're watertight.

If you're using corn ear leaves, take one and wrap it lengthwise around the tamale. Tie some string around each of the ends, so it looks like a strange green Christmas cracker. If there are gaps in the middle, take another leaf and wrap it around the middle, then tie that one with another piece of string. If you're using baking paper, wrap them in that. Either way, make sure that the wrapping overlaps with itself to keep all the dough covered. Follow the same procedure with the remaining tamales.

Put the tamales into a steamer or colander over a saucepan of boiling water and steam them, over a medium heat, for about 20 minutes. Try serving these tamales with peperoncino on the side, a lovely Sicilian chilli pepper tapenade sold in Fresh & Wild's condiments section.

LAWRENCE **CAKE**

Lawrence, one of my two lovely nephews, has a very kooky sense of taste. Contrary to popular belief, lots of very young children like Lawrence love strong, fresh flavours. It's only when they get to the school playground that they start conforming more and saying things like 'I don't like it'. Give little ones olives and strawberries if you want to see them smile and just check out that dimple-factor when they're munching garlic, onions and leeks.

I developed this cake to celebrate Lawrence's love of all things allium. It's surprisingly sweet if the leeks are caramelized well, but is definitely a savoury lunch dish and not a dessert. The sun-dried tomatoes make it a pretty salty cake, with the poppy seeds matching the earthy oniony taste, and the herbs and spices supporting the central allium zing.

To grow garlic chives, simply make some clove-sized dents in a pot of soil, sprinkle a little sand inside the holes, then put a clove of garlic into each, root-end down, and cover with soil. Crop the shoots when they're about 10–15cm high. More shoots will keep coming, so you can make more cakes or add the snipped shoots to salads or hot dishes to give them a lovely 'chivesy' flavour.

Kuzu root is a natural thickener that has been used in Japanese and Chinese cooking for the last 2000 years. It looks a bit like chalk. The gravel-sized lumps can be dissolved directly in water or ground in a suribachi before use. A suribachi is a rough stoneware bowl in which you grind foods with a surikogi. It's basically a pestle and mortar, but better, as the bowl is rough inside so you can get a more effective grinding action.

A suribachi and surikogi set is great if you plan to grind kuzu, as this chalk-like root will ruin your coffee grinder. They've got them at Fresh & Wild, imported from Japan by Clearspring, the same company that supply the jars of kuzu. Alternatively, just mash the kuzu in a bowl with the back of a metal spoon, and use your suribachi to grind fresh ginger and garlic.

Kuzu root does pretty much the same job as cornflour and costs a lot more for pretty much the same thickening power. However, whilst corn-flour is low on nutritional value and healing properties, dried kuzu root is really good for you. In the Far East, people use kuzu in the same way that echinacea is used in the West. As well as helping prevent colds, it's also good for your tummy, eases back and shoulder cramps, and is even good for hangovers. Not bad for a humble cake ingredient.

Rapadura is simply sugar cane juice that's been evaporated to leave unrefined sugar. The difference is that rapadura is a kind of sugar that's still rich in micro-nutrients, with a pleasantly toffee-ish flavour and less sickly sticky sweetness.

The beetroot and carrots in this recipe add a bit of sweetness, a bit of texture and a lot of colour. Wear washing-up gloves when you grate the beetroot, or wash your hands in cold water straight afterwards. Serve with Root Salad (see page 216) or a really herby tabbouleh salad.

LAWRENCE **CAKE**

75g sun-dried tomatoes (the dry ones, not in oil)

175ml goat's milk

2 medium leeks

150ml olive oil

1 tablespoon finely chopped garlic chives

1 tablespoon blue poppy seeds

1 teaspoon dried marjoram

1 teaspoon dried thyme

1 teaspoon dried rosemary

1 tablespoon rapadura

300g spelt flour

30g kuzu, powdered

1¼ teaspoons baking powder

150g butter, cold and diced

30g olives with stones, pitted and finely chopped

1 small carrot, grated

1 medium beetroot, grated

3 eggs

120ml goat's yogurt

Put the sun-dried tomatoes in a small dish, cover with the goat's milk and leave to soak for at least a couple of hours, but, if possible, overnight in the fridge. When you're ready to begin cooking, preheat the oven to 180°C/350°F/Gas Mark 4.

Chop the roots and the very tops off the leeks, then slit them down their lengths and chop into 2cm-ish chunks. Put the chopped leeks into a colander and rinse thoroughly in cold water. Put the colander over a large saucepan of boiling water on a medium heat, cover and steam for a few minutes.

Heat a tablespoon of the oil in a large frying pan or wok, over a high heat, then fry the leeks, garlic chives, poppy seeds, herbs and the rapadura, stirring them with a wooden spoon. The mixture should caramelize quickly, but make sure it doesn't burn. Take the pan off the heat.

In a big bowl, mix the flour, kuzu and baking powder, then throw in the butter. With your cold fingers, lightly rub the butter into the flour to make crumbs. Strain the goat's milk into another bowl and set aside. Chop the soaked tomatoes roughly with scissors, then add them to the flour. Now add the leek mixture, olives, carrot and beetroot to the flour as well.

Break the eggs into the milk, add the yogurt and olive oil, then whisk well. Pour this liquid into the flour bowl little by little, stirring as you do. Slowly combine all the ingredients in this way to form a thick batter. Spoon the mixture into a well-oiled 25cm-round cake tin, preferably with a loose bottom to make it easier to get the cake out. Put the cake tin onto a baking sheet, just in case.

Bake the cake for about 50 minutes. It's done when a metal knife, inserted into the middle of the cake, comes out clean – and when your kitchen is full of herby caramelized onion smells. Serve the cake hot, or leave it to cool on a wire rack and serve cold.

ON A ROLL ...

Nori Sushi Wraps

Sushi are the sandwiches of Japan. It's the same concept of a starchy grain plus a filling, only instead of bread it's rice.

The key to making sushi is to use the best quality and freshest ingredients. After that, it's all child's play – so long as you have your trusty sushi mat. These are made from lengths of thinly split bamboo, woven together with string. They don't cost much and are an essential tool for this easy, tasty dish.The vinegar, mirin, syrup and ume plum seasoning make up the vinegar dressing in this recipe but, if you want, you can use Clearspring's ready-mixed Sushi Vinegar instead. Personally, I think it's more fun to make your own, and you can use the individual ingredients in other dishes, from stir-fries to vinaigrettes.

Nori is a type of seaweed that's been pressed into flat sheets in exactly the same way as hand-made paper. The seaweed used for nori-making is grown on rope nets that are suspended between long bamboo poles set deep in Japanese bays where the currents are gentle. Very slowly, the nori begins to grow over the winter until it covers the net, ready for harvesting in late January and February. It's hand-picked from the sea and brought ashore, then washed in fresh water and made into sheets.

ON A ROLL ...

Nori Sushi Wraps

MAKES 8 ROLLS:

250g short grain brown rice

2 teaspoons brown rice vinegar

1 teaspoon mirin

1 teaspoon brown rice malt syrup

1 teaspoon ume plum seasoning

4 tablespoons toasted sesame seeds

¼ a cucumber

1 big carrot, scrubbed

2 spring onions

2 sheets nori or 2 sheets pre-toasted sushi nori

Some takuan/pickled daikon

Some sushi ginger

Some sushi garlic

FOR DIPPING:

1 teaspoon wasabi powder

Tamari

Gomasio

Boil the rice until cooked, drain it, place it back in the pan and cover to keep it warm. In a cup, mix the vinegar, mirin, malt syrup and ume plum seasoning with a fork. Throw the sesame seeds into the rice pan. Pour a little bit of the vinegar dressing onto the rice, then toss the rice with salad serving spoons. Repeat this process until the rice is well coated and the dressing is all gone. Leave the rice to absorb the vinegar with the lid on.

Meanwhile, slice the cucumber and carrot into julienne strips. This simply means cutting off the tops and tails, slicing the veg lengthwise, then thinly to make big matchsticks. Remove the roots from the spring onions plus any dodgy ends, then slice in half lengthwise. Slice again finely so you have long shreds or spring onion.

If you're using standard non-toasted nori, now is the time to toast it. Do this by simply dangling it about 10cm over the gas flame or electric burner on your hob. It'll turn golden metallic green (yes, honestly!). You're now ready to use the sushi mat. Using scissors, cut the nori sheets into four quarters. Cover the top half of the mat with a sheet of nori, then pile on a sixteenth of the rice. Spread it out, leaving 2cm of nori clear of any filling at the bottom edge.

Arrange the vegetables and Japanese pickles of your choice on top, then cover with another sixteenth of the rice. Moisten the bare piece of nori so that it'll stick to itself. Carefully roll the mat as tightly as possible around the rice, being careful that you don't lose the end of the mat under itself. Squeeze the roll so that it sticks to itself, then put it onto a flat plate. Repeat the process until you have used all the nori and filling.

Serve with a saucer of wasabi powder mixed with water, a dish of tamari and a sprinkling of gomasio for dipping.

HAM GRAM FLAN

Ready-made pastry falls into a similar category as ready-grated Cheddar cheese or ready-chopped broccoli florets. We can't quite quantify how such things make our lives better, yet many of us still seem to buy these time-saving, money-spending options.

Personally, I'd rather save money by avoiding such 'convenient' products and instead pay out the extra cash on better ingredients. Spending a few minutes on pastry making, cheese grating and broccoli 'floret-ing' makes me feel nice after a long day working. And if you really want to save time, simply make your pastry in a food processor.

The exception to the convenience rule is puff pastry, which takes forever and generally tastes pretty good out of the freezer – so long as it's organic. Non-organic puff pastry is full of hydrogenated fats, which are particularly artery clogging and heart-attack-inducing. This stuff is also often added to non-organic biscuits and the like. It looks for all the world like little white plastic ball-bearings, and if you were to hold it in your hand all day, it wouldn't melt. It's much too hard for that. Much harder than any fat in nature, in fact, as it's had an extra hydrogen molecule added precisely to achieve this kind of strength.

It's added not through evilness, but practicality – dunk a biscuit containing hydrogenated fats and the soggy bottom half will stay intact all the way to your mouth. The only trouble is, once you've eaten the biscuit, the hydrogenated fat is rejected by your body as an alien substance and, unless your kidneys and liver are feeling particularly zealous, the fat is laid out into a micro-thin coating inside your arteries. To my mind, I'd prefer to lessen the time between the dunk and the mouth dash, rather than risk artery fuzz.

Anyway, back to the quiche. It's made with gram flour, which is simply ground up chickpeas. These have the added benefit of helping ward off osteoporosis with their high levels of calcium and phyto-oestrogens.

Personally, I love flours with gluten in them, such as wheat flour, just as much as those without. Sensible helpings of wheat within a nicely varied diet seems like a good idea to me, unless you've been diagnosed with coeliac disease. But eating wheaty toast for breakfast, wheaty sandwiches for lunch, a wheaty cake at teatime and wheaty pasta for dinner isn't a good idea. It's all a case of using a bit of common, and being aware of what you're putting inside your body.

The culinary reason this quiche is made with gram flour is so that it doesn't rise. It produces a compact, crispy pastry that's ideal for holding the filling without going soggy. It tastes pretty much the same as regular pastry, although it's more crumbly in a delicate and really delicious biscuity way. And it's great to have the added chickpea phyto-nutrients and protein, which help make this a totally top tart.

Enjoy it hot or cold, with seasonal leaves or Balsamic Beets salad (see page 233).

HAM GRAM FLAN

MAKES A QUICHE FOR 2:

FOR THE PASTRY:

150g gram flour

75g soft butter

1–2 tablespoons cold water

FOR THE FILLING:

200g sheep's feta

A slice of ham (optional)

100g fresh big spinach leaves, washed and thick stems removed

1 small red onion, peeled

2 garlic cloves, peeled

A handful of fresh flat-leaf parsley

1 medium-sized ripe tomato

A dozen black olives

2 tablespoons olive oil

2 eggs

Crushed black pepper to taste

Make the pastry by using cold fingers to mix the flour and butter in a bowl. Let the mixture fall through your fingers as you lightly rub it – and enjoy the sensation. Alternatively, stick the ingredients in a food processor and zap. Either way, when it resembles breadcrumbs, mix in the water and lightly knead it into a ball. Wrap it in a clean plastic carrier bag and set it aside for half an hour.

Meanwhile, finely chop the feta, ham, spinach, onion, garlic and parsley into little individual piles. Slice the tomato on its side, and pit the olives. In a large frying pan, heat the oil, add the onion and fry on a medium heat for a couple of minutes. Throw in the garlic, spinach and a tablespoon of cold water, put the lid on and reduce the heat. Take the pan off the heat after a couple more minutes. Pour this spinach mixture into a bowl with the other chopped ingredients and the olives, but not the tomato. Crack the eggs into the bowl and then stir everything.

Grease an 18cm loose-bottom round flan tin, and preheat the oven to 180°C/350°F/Gas Mark 4. Take the pastry dough out of the bag and roll it out on a floured surface. It will break up a bit, but don't worry. Press it into the tin, lining the bottom and sides, and trimming and pressing to make a nicely fitting layer of pastry.

Pour in the filling mixture, sprinkle on the pepper and then place the tomato slices on top. Bake in the oven for about 30 minutes, then test if the egg looks set. If not, give it another 5–10 minutes.

CORAL'S **KASHA**

Coral is my mum and kasha is traditional eastern European roasted buckwheat. They're a great combination. Buckwheat originally came from China, spreading across Asia and the Middle East into Eastern Europe with the Crusaders a thousand years ago. It's now a staple part of Russian and Polish cuisine.

Buckwheat tastes a bit nutty and is cute, with little triangular grains. It's a rich, starchy whole grain that is high in the B vitamin group that's so good for memory and general brain power. Buckwheat is also a gentle mood tonic, as it contains a compound called rutin that helps the body deal with stress. It's handy to keep you hardy during the colder months of our Northern European island home, as it tones up the tiniest capillaries to become more resistant to frostbite and keeps broken veins at bay later in life.

You can sprout buckwheat grain really successfully at home to use as part of a salad sandwich filling, or mill the grain into flour for traditional Russian Blintzes (see page 12). You can buy buckwheat either plain or roasted. The roasted grain is labelled in the UK by its Polish name, kasha, or simply as roasted buckwheat.

In this recipe, the whole roasted grains are cooked up simply, to make a lovely warm winter lunch, or a cold summer grain salad. You can also serve it as a side dish with your dinner, instead of rice or potatoes.

CORAL'S **KASHA**

2 tablespoons olive oil

1 large or 2 small onions, peeled and diced

1 medium carrot, scrubbed and diced

4 white or chestnut mushrooms, sliced

200g roasted buckwheat

1 egg, beaten

500ml boiling water

Heat the oil in a frying pan, over a medium heat, add the onions and carrots and fry for 5 minutes, stirring with a wooden spoon. Add the mushrooms, cover the pan, turn the heat down, and leave to gently sauté.

Wash the grain in cold water, then drain well. Heat the buckwheat in a deep frying pan, over a low heat, stirring with the spoon. Pour the egg over the grain and stir it in quickly to stop the egg scrambling. The idea is that it will coat the grains and keep them separate.

Pour the water in, put the lid on the pan and simmer for 10–15 minutes, or until the buckwheat is tender. Check every now and then that the pan hasn't run dry, adding a little more water if necessary. When the grain is cooked, add the cooked vegetables, mix well and serve.

TEMPEH, TSUYU, CARROT

and Alfalfa Pittas

Tempeh (pronounced *tem-pay*) is an Indonesian delicacy made out of fermented soy beans. Local cooks boil up soy beans, add a bacterial culture, press the mixture into blocks and leave it to ferment. The process sounds kinda revolting, until you compare the process to Western cheese-making techniques. Believe me – it's gorgeous stuff.

Tempeh has a rich mushroom-like flavour that is a million miles away from the blandness of tofu.

And tempeh contains about twenty times as many isoflavones as tofu, which are the natural substances that give soy foods their anti-cancer properties and help promote a healthy heart. In this recipe it is steam-fried in oils and tamari, but it is equally at home in anything from a bolognaise-style sauce to a curry.

Look for it in the fridge, plain, marinated or with added flavours, in the freezer, or in jars in the Japanese section of the store with sea vegetables or in sauces. I keep some in the house at all times, ready for super-quick meals, either for lunch or dinner. Tempeh's natural flavour is enhanced by tsuyu, a shoyu-based brown liquid made with concentrated shiitake mushrooms.

Alfalfa is an Arabic word meaning 'father of all foods'. If you let the sprouts grow big, they'll become deep-rooting bushy plants. Fat chance of that happening though, because once you discover these curly little sprouts they'll be straight in your sandwich.

Alfalfa sprouts are sold in bags in the fresh produce display, plus the dried starter seeds can be found in paper packets next to the pulses. Alfalfa sprouts contain five of the eight essential amino acids, making them a nutritionally balanced food. They've also got lots of trace minerals that you won't get from many other foods, plus a whole bunch of vitamins, including lots of stress-busting B vitamins. They help your body's immune system, aiding natural detoxification of the blood and helping the general digestive process. And they're crunchy, too! Check out the recipe on page 262 for Essene Bread, where you'll find the method for sprouting your own seeds.

TEMPEH, TSUYU, CARROT

and Alfalfa Pittas

TO MAKE 4 PITTAS FOR 2 PEOPLE'S LUNCHES:

1 teaspoon sunflower oil
1 teaspoon sesame oil
200g plain tempeh, sliced like cheese
3 tablespoons tsuyu
2 small and sweet carrots, scrubbed
1 bag alfalfa sprouts
4 tablespoons tahini
4 pitta breads
Butter

Heat the oils in a shallow frying pan over a medium heat. Add the tempeh and fry for a couple of minutes on both sides, then drop in 1 tablespoon of the tsuyu, which will sizzle. Put the lid on the pan and turn the heat down low.

Meanwhile, grate the carrots into a bowl. Rinse the alfalfa and shake it loads to get rid of excess water. Put it onto a clean tea towel to absorb excess water. Mix the tahini and the last 2 tablespoons of tsuyu in a saucer, then add some cold water little by little to make a smooth and runny sauce. Put the pittas into your toaster on a medium setting and wait for them to ping.

Check how the tempeh is doing. It should be cooked in about 5 minutes from start to finish. When it is, slice open the hot pittas and butter them inside. Stuff them with the tempeh slices, the grated carrots and the alfalfa. Drizzle the filling with the tahini sauce and serve immediately.

COD'S ROE **FAJITAS**

Invented by the original Mexican cowboys of America, fajitas are tortillas filled with marinated beef, guacamole and salad. That makes this recipe a contradiction in terms, as fajitas are by definition made from beef by guys who raise cows. It's like making shepherd's pie out of minced beef instead of lamb – think about it … Oh well, these surf fajitas taste just as fab as turf fajitas. And we're a long way from Mexico so let's bend the rules.

I'm hearing confusion at the back – yes, I did say that the original cowboys came from Mexico. The cigarette pack version of the blond all-American cowboy is a myth, along with Custer's last stand and a million and one other Hollywood enhancements of American history. Cowboys were Spanish-speaking migrant workers from south of the border, and it was many decades before they were joined by a wider population of men – amongst them former slaves from the plantations and unemployed ex-Confederate soldiers left homeless after the war. The original cowboys were actually called vaqueros, and were based on ranchos which were established to convert the local Indians to Catholicism and the Spanish way of life. The advent of the railroads in the 1860s meant that beef could be sent to the rich eastern coast of America and hence things went crazy. A vast amount of cattle was then moved, and wild buffalo herds were mercilessly hunted to near extinction, all within a brief twenty-five-year period. Anyway, back to the point – by all accounts, cowboys made a mean fajita.

Despite its availability throughout the year elsewhere, cod's roe is only actually in season from January until February, so make this dish during this brief window of opportunity. That's what makes foods special, eating them at specific times when they're in season in your neck of the woods. So if you see cod's roe on sale in another store in December, you'll know that it's been frozen for nearly a year.

Watch out for proper fresh smoked cod's roe taramasalata at this time, too – it's made by the Cornish fishermen who catch Fresh & Wild's cod. During the rest of the year, replace the cod's roe in this recipe with crayfish tails or fish like brill, whiting or John Dory, or simply freeze up a batch of cod's roe at home if you want to prolong the season and eat it in spring – you naughty ...

COD'S ROE **FAJITAS**

FOR LUNCH FOR 6:

500g raw cod's roe

1 ear of fresh sweetcorn or a small tin of sweetcorn

1 tablespoon olive oil

1 medium red onion, peeled and finely chopped

12 pods of fresh peas, shelled or a handful of frozen peas, defrosted

3 garlic cloves, peeled and crushed

1 red pepper, deseeded and chopped

1 yellow pepper, deseeded and chopped

2 big ripe tomatoes, diced

1 fresh red chilli, halved, deseeded and membranes removed

2 tablespoons Worcestershire sauce

1 big ripe avocado or 2 small ones

4 sprigs coriander, finely chopped

Juice of a freshly-squeezed lemon

1 jar Sicilian pepperoncino

1 pot plain cow's, sheep's, goat's or soy yogurt

12 caribe chilli tortillas (see recipe on page 252)

Wrap your lump of cod's roe tightly in foil, covering it a few times to ensure that the parcel is watertight. Put the ball of foil into a large saucepan of boiling water, cover with a lid and boil for 20 minutes. Remove the parcel and unwrap the foil, being careful not to burn your fingers. Slice the cooked roe.

Remove the outer leaves from the fresh sweetcorn if that's what you're using. Put the leaves in a paper bag and stick them in the fridge for Tomorrow's Tamales (see page 42). With a small sharp knife, cut off the corn kernels, cutting as close to the woody inside stem as possible to avoid wasting the corn. If you don't have fresh ears of corn, open the tin of sweetcorn and drain.

Heat the oil in a cast iron char-grilling pan, or a medium frying pan, over a medium heat. When it's warm, throw in the corn, onion and peas, and cook for a couple of minutes. Then add the cod's roe slices, garlic, peppers, tomatoes, half the fresh chilli and the Worcestershire sauce. Turn the heat down to low and cook for about 5 more minutes, turning the fish roe and vegetables now and then so that they char, caramelize and cook, but don't burn.

Meanwhile, prepare the avocado. With a sharp knife, cut through the skin right down to the stone and slice along the length of the fruit around the whole circumference. Twist the two halves in opposite directions so the avocado opens into two halves. Remove the stone and slice the flesh with the back of your knife through to the skin, but don't cut the skin. Do this again the opposite way to make cubes, which you can easily remove from the skin with your fingers. Put the diced avocado flesh into a bowl and squash it with a fork. Add the remaining half of the chilli, the coriander and the lemon juice, and squash together some more.

Put the guacamole on the table, along with the jar of pepperoncino and the pot of yogurt. If you're feeling fancy, you could spoon them into nice bowls instead. Tip the cod's roe and vegetable mixture into a nice big bowl and put that out, too, plus the warm tortillas. Make sure there are lots of spoons so everyone can help themselves. Let everyone put whatever fillings they want onto their tortilla and roll them themselves for messy, spicy finger food.

PS If you've freshly made your tortillas, then they'll be nice and warm and ready to roll. If your tortillas have been sitting in the fridge, put them onto a plate over a saucepan of boiling water, cover with a tea towel and heat for 10 minutes.

SLOW ROASTED GARLICKY TOMATOES

with Tymsboro' Cheese and Watercress

This is a lunch idea for all those lucky people who don't go out to work. Freelances, mums, people recovering from an illness, and students are the main ones that come to mind. Being at home means you can easily whack the tomatoes in the oven around about the time you break for elevenses. That way, when lunchtime comes, you'll be eating a culinary delicacy without having to lift a finger.

Tymsboro' is a fantastic artisan-made English goat's cheese, dusted in salt and charcoal and shaped like a pyramid without the top. It's pretty exciting, because it's liquid around the edges, but is harder inside, which gives it a great contrast and balance of consistency. It is, however, unpasteurized so pregnant women will have to skip this one until the bun is out the oven. The rest of you can read on ...

It's an unpasteurized and seasonal cheese, as the maker believes in doing things the old way. Mary Holbrook makes the cheese at Sleight Farm, in the Mendips, just south of Bath. She's got together a flock of naughty goats that are three ancient heirloom breeds: British Saanen, British Alpine and Anglo-Nubian goats. Not only are they well suited to life in the Mendips, they make great tasting milk with just the right amount of fat to make creamy Tymsboro' cheese.

And they're all naughty because, being goats, they just can't help it. There are about 90 goats in Mary's flock and there's nothing they like better than running away. It's not that they don't like life at Sleight Farm, it's just that they love being bad. They're fussy eaters, too, who prefer nettles and thistles to lots of grass. But they're in luck, because Mary's fields are full of wild weeds and meadow flowers instead of the usual mono-culture of grass, grass and more grass. This isn't just out of kindness to her goats. Mary knows that a mixture of wild plants in their diet means lovely fragrant milk for her cheeses.

Mary basically adopted the French method for making traditional charcoal-coated goat's cheese, then developed it and made it her own. She uses the very freshest goat's milk to start off the cheese-making process – it's never any older than milk that's been milked from the goats the night before. That's why the cheese is seasonal, as the goats like making milk from spring through to autumn, resting up over the winter in nice cosy straw-lined barns.

To get the cheese-making process going, Mary gently heats the milk (but doesn't pasteurize it), adds a culture and a tiny bit of rennet, then leaves the liquid for 24 hours to make a soft curd. This is where the real skill and cheese-making flair comes in, because the way you handle this delicate curd will deeply affect the final flavour of the cheese. It's fragile stuff, as the fat globules in the goat's milk are small and easily broken, spoiling the cheese's consistency, too. This is also what makes goat's milk more easily digestible by people than cow's milk.

So slowly and very carefully, the curds are spooned into the moulds, ready to be matured over the next three to four weeks. Penicillin in the ripening room's air naturally makes a beeline for the little pyramids, finishing the maturing process. The cheeses are then turned out of the moulds and dusted with salt and charcoal ready to be sent to us.

But why pyramids without tops? It's another French thing ... Apparently Napoleon was sitting by a traditional French pyramid-shaped goat's cheese when he was told that his army hadn't managed to invade and conquer Egypt. His first reaction was to chop off the top of the pyramid in an act of defiance – bet that taught the pesky Egyptians who was boss.

The finished Tymsboro' cheese has an **almondy-lemony flavour**, which the acidity of the slow-roasted tomatoes sets off perfectly.

And if you make more slow-roasted tomatoes than you need, you can store them in jars filled with olive oil ready for next time.

Fresh & Wild's watercress is grown by John Hurd at his farm in Wiltshire. John's been growing watercress for over 50 years, so what he doesn't know about it can be written on a stamp. It's one of the most difficult salad crops to grow, as it's not grown in soil like most other plants. Instead, watercress is grown in shallow trays filled with a precise mixture of layered gravels and sands. These beds are then flooded with freshly drawn spring water from the freshwater springs deep in the chalky Wiltshire grounds of the farm, with up to half a million gallons of spring water flowing through each acre every day.

John invented the techniques needed to grow watercress organically on a large enough scale to supply shops. Previously, large-scale watercress farms in the UK routinely used copious amounts of molluscicides, pesticides that are designed to specifically kill slugs and snails. In fact, non-organic watercress farms still do, hence non-organic watercress is one of the most pesticide-rich crops you can buy.

Slugs and snails would love to live in John's organic watercress trays and munch our tasty peppery greens, but he's worked out a way to keep the trays snail and slug free without resorting to poisonous chemicals. This is a real breakthrough, as watercress farms were plagued in the 1910s and 1920s with a type of snail that passes on liver fluke to the people that eat it. John Hurd's meticulous organic cleansing methods ensure that the organic watercress we eat today is free of both nasty molluscicides and potentially sickness-causing beasties.

The strong peppery taste of watercress is a real wake-up call to the senses, and it's full of get-up-and-go vitamins, too. As John says: 'Watercress contains more vitamin C than fresh oranges and more calcium than cow's milk.' It's also packed with zinc, magnesium and vitamins B6 and E, plus the beta-carotene and iron that our bodies synthesize into vitamin A. The balance of these vitamins is causing a stir in the cancer healing community, as they're proven to protect from, and help reverse, free-radical damage. Watercress has also been proclaimed an aphrodisiac since ancient times. Get it on.

SLOW ROASTED GARLICKY TOMATOES

with Tymsboro' Cheese and Watercress

LUNCH FOR 2:

6 medium-sized ripe tomatoes
3 garlic cloves, peeled and thinly sliced
A knob of butter
1 Tymsboro' cheese
A bunch of John Hurd's watercress
Olive oil, to taste
A handful of walnut pieces, to taste

Preheat the oven to 130°C/250°F/Gas Mark 1/2. Cut the tomatoes along their lengths and put them on a baking sheet, cut side up. Put a couple of slices of garlic on top of each half, then roast for about 3 hours. Take them out of the oven and remove the garlic.

Put the grill on full power. Slice the Tymsboro' into 0.5cm thick squares and butter the widest side, apart from the top one, which should be buttered on the crust. Put the cheese slices onto a baking tray, buttered side down, and grill for about 3 or 4 minutes, until they're bubbling and have gone golden brown.

Serve the tomatoes with the Tymsboro' cheese and a bowl of freshly-cut watercress, drizzled with olive oil to taste and scattered with walnuts. Put some Quinoa Grissini (see page 254) on the table too, plus some decent bread.

CHEEKY CHILLI **CHOCOLATE MUSHROOMS**

There's a lot of confusion about whether or not chocolate is good for you. Some people feel that it's natural, so it's gotta be good for you. Well, sort of, but then again, lots of natural things aren't healthy, like tobacco and tarantulas. On the plus side, cocoa is high on the polyphenol antioxidants that protect you from cancer. And it's high in the phenylethylamine chemicals released by your brain when you fall in love. It's got lots of iron and magnesium, too, which may be why women often crave good dark chocolate when the moon is full.

On the downside, cocoa also has a lot of caffeine in it and contains another stimulant called theobromine. And almost all chocolate bars are stuffed with saturated fat and sugar. Of course, organic chocolate is a zillion times better than dodgy mass market brands, and is the best way of guaranteeing that you don't eat artery-clogging hydrogenated fats.

On balance, the feel-good factor generated by the phenylethylamines makes great quality cocoa an acceptable part of a happy and balanced diet – which is lucky, 'cause I know y'all would ignore me if I said you shouldn't eat it.

This savoury cocoa recipe will help wean you off the chocolate bars. Don't grimace – savoury was the original way with cocoa; the one and only way for the Aztecs who invented cocoa powder. Just try this dish – it works. You'll soon be liberally scattering cocoa onto lots of savoury numbers in your kitchen. It's particularly good when paired with robust flavours like red meats and earthy vegetables. Cooked with chilli, it's a marriage made in heaven. So maybe you could eat a few less chocolate bars containing sugar and supplement with your new-found savoury cocoa numbers in between.

On the chilli front, there are conflicting opinions again about their healthiness. But one thing's for sure – they stimulate the release of the same happiness endorphins as cocoa. That's why when you eat some really hot chillies, you can't bear the heat, but you find yourself going back for more a few seconds later. It's addictive stuff that makes you feel good. It's also high in vitamin C, although Ayurvedic principles say that some people should go easy. Try telling that to the Aztecs.

And on the mushroom front, any old mushroom will do, which is exactly what Portabella (or Portobello) mushrooms are. They're simply mature button mushrooms – ones that have been left to develop their flavour to the max, with a beefy texture to match.

CHEEKY CHILLI **CHOCOLATE** **MUSHROOMS**

LUNCH FOR 1:

2 big open Portabella mushrooms
1 small fresh red chilli pepper
1 teaspoon toasted sesame oil
1 tablespoon sunflower oil
1 heaped teaspoon cocoa powder
2 slices of good bread
Butter to spread

Slice the mushrooms and set them aside. Slice open the chilli, remove and discard the white membranes and seeds, and finely chop the chilli. As chilli juice stings, you might want to wear washing-up gloves to do this, particularly if you're likely to rub your eyes or any other sensitive places at some point in the near future.

Heat the oils in a frying pan on a medium heat. Add the cocoa and as much chilli as you think you'd like to eat, and fry for 1 minute, stirring with a wooden spoon. Now add the mushrooms, lower the heat and put the lid on the pan.

Put the bread in the toaster and hit go. Give the mushrooms a stir and then put the lid back on. When the toast pings, butter it and if the mushrooms are soft and meltingly ready, place them on top, serve and enjoy.

TOTALLY SHELLFISH...

Steamed Scallops, Clams, Cockles and Mussels

This fresh, seaside-inspired, quick-to-cook lunch features seafood in a white wine broth, fragranced with spring onions, garlic and ginger. All the seafood ingredients are local, with scallops, mussels and cockles from Cornwall, and clams from France. Most shellfish sellers seem to make you buy their wares a kilo at a time, but Fresh & Wild let you buy smaller amounts, making it possible to mix together different varieties without having lots left over.

Most scallops are farmed these days, but some are dredged by trawlers using huge nets. Farmed scallops often don't taste that great, while dredging with huge industrial nets catches everything else on the seabed, destroying a lot of the marine ecosystem in the process. This leaves two other options – diver-caught scallops or scallops dredged with small nets. Both of these options are available from Fresh & Wild.

Scallops are made up of two parts: the scallop itself and the coral. The big white round scallop bit is actually the abductor muscle, which the scallop uses to open and close its pretty shell. The other little coral bit is in fact the roe, which is creamy white for boy scallops and orange for the girls.

Clams come in various different sub-species, including carpet shell clams, surf clams, razor clams and warty venus clams (I kid you not). They all like to live about half a metre under the sand, where they sit all day and all night, filtering water for microscopic food and oxygen. That really is about it, apart from when the females spout eggs, the males spout sperms, and the little larvae that result swim about until they find a nice spot to sit for the rest of their lives, filtering all that water.

The tastiest little clams are generally agreed to be manila clams, which are also known as short-necked clams. North American cherrystone clams are also pretty delicious and they're starting to breed them here in the UK.

Cockles are one of the smallest beasties available at Fresh & Wild, along with the tiny ready-cooked brown shrimps sold in packets in the fridge.

We're generally offered hand-picked, dredged, or tractor-harvested cockles. The cockle-picking tragedy at Morecambe Bay highlighted the terrible conditions that some cockle-pickers have to endure, so you'll be relieved to know that ethical sources of cockles do exist in this country. Fresh & Wild's cockles come from Burry Inlet in south-west Wales, and cockle-picking here is approved by the Marine Stewardship Council.

People have been cockle-picking here since the 1800s and they still use the same method today as their predecessors did then. The sand flats have never been dredged. The wet sand is raked by hand and then sieved to find the little cockles, which are about 5cm in diameter. The cockle-pickers carry a little ruler thingy called a riddle so they can make sure that all the cockles they collect are big enough to be adults.

Originally, all the cockle-pickers of Burry Inlet were women, who collected wild cockles whilst their men-folk went down the mines. Nowadays, cockle-pickers are from both genders, and they have to be licensed to collect the cockles. This ensures that the cockles – and the pickers – are protected. People are only allowed to gather a maximum of 300 kilos per day and no collection is ever allowed by night. Burry Inlet is checked regularly by two different marine councils to make sure that the cockle-pickers are fine, and that the cockles stay at good sustainable stock levels.

Mussels are usually farmed these days, either locally or on distant shores, with green-lipped mussels being flown into the UK from as far afield as New Zealand. Farming means hanging ropes out at sea, seeding them and then waiting for the molluscs to grow. Fresh & Wild, as you might expect, sells fresh and wild mussels. These are from a regulated area off the coast of Cornwall, where the mussels have been clinging to rocks and each other using sticky threads they've made themselves. And they taste much richer than most farmed ones.

All of the shellfish in this recipe are bivalve molluscs, which means they're in season from September until April – hence the old saying about only eating shellfish when there's an 'r' in the month. That said, they're at their tastiest at the beginning of their season and at their cheapest at the end of the season. Time to get messy ...

TOTALLY SHELLFISH...

Steamed Scallops, Clams, Cockles and Mussels

LUNCH FOR 4:

1 tablespoon olive oil

1 tablespoon sesame oil

4 spring onions, trimmed and finely chopped

4 garlic cloves, peeled and finely chopped

4cm piece ginger root, grated

300ml white wine

A dozen shell-less scallops, rinsed

500g mussels, scrubbed

500g clams, scrubbed

500g cockles, scrubbed

Finely chopped sushi ginger, to taste

Finely chopped chives, to taste

Begin by tapping each individual open shell on the side of your saucepan. If it doesn't close, throw it away.

Heat the oils in a big saucepan over a low heat, then add the spring onions, garlic and ginger when the oil is hot. Put the lid on and sauté for about 5 minutes. Add the wine and turn the heat up to medium. Bring the liquid to the boil, then put the scallops into a colander and suspend it over the pan. Put the lid over the scallops.

After about 4 minutes, pick the colander up with oven gloves and throw the mussels and clams into the saucepan. Put the colander of scallops back over the pan immediately and keep cooking. Two minutes later, lift the colander with oven gloves again and throw in the cockles. Put the colander back onto the pan, hold the lid tightly and shake the pan really well. Put the pan back on the heat and keep cooking.

Two minutes later, turn the heat off, take the colander off the pan and put it onto a plate. Take the lid off the scallops and put it back onto the saucepan. Wearing oven gloves and holding the lid tightly, shake the saucepan again.

Open the lid, pick out any shellfish that are still tightly closed and throw them away. Divide the rest between four suitably-sized bowls and place three scallops on top of each serving. Sprinkle some sushi ginger and chives over each scallop.

Serve with little finger bowls of warm water with a slice of lemon floating in each one, and eat the shellfish using an empty mussel shell as pincer chopsticks.

SMÖRGÅSBORD

This isn't a recipe as such, but a suggestion to inspire your curiosity. Lots of countries operate the smörgåsbord principle, from the classic English picnic to the Moroccan tagine and salads spread. Smörgåsbord is a Swedish word – *smörgås* meaning 'open sandwich' and *bord* meaning 'table'. The idea, however, remains the same the world over – a spread of lots of foods from which guests can choose helpings of whatever they wish.

What you'll need is some decent bread, a platter of cold meats, a bunch of cold and marinated fish, a board of fine cheeses, a few different salads, some cold cooked vegetables and a gaggle of flavoursome sauces and pastes.

It goes without saying, but choose your bread with care. Standard, soft sliced stuff was one of the very first fast foods to become established in industrialized countries, which is why it's so ubiquitous. The cheapest grain is used, it's mixed with way too much yeast so that it rises as quick as is biologically possible and then it's flash-baked for only a few minutes to save on costs. This stuff is basically sold unbaked, which is why when you squash it together with your fingers it turns back into something very similar to raw dough. The starches in the grain haven't metabolized, the yeast is still active and the flavour and texture you know all about.

Decent bread on the other hand – that's a whole meal in itself. Whether baked in your kitchen, or baked by a reputable bakery, it's one of those things that you know is worth having every day. The Village Bakery in Cumbria supply unusual breads to Fresh & Wild, like their Brazil Nut and Linseed Loaf, or their Maize, Chestnut and Lupin Bread. Hobbs House Bakery in Gloucestershire makes traditional rustic loaves, such as Wild Rye or Spelt breads, and Flour Power in London bake Fresh & Wild's everyday breads, like full-flavoured, crusty wholemeal cobs and traditional aromatic white baguettes. So what's the secret ingredient in any decent loaf? As with so many things, it's time.

Now you've got your loaf sorted, how about the cold meats? Choose from a **stunning array of hams and salamis**, cured beef and smoked venison.

Try Prima Vera's Italian Parma ham and Sicilian mortadella, Malone's Irish whiskey salami or Islay's Scottish smoked beef. Or any of the other slow-cured, marinated or smoked cold meats on the deli counter.

And while you're there, choose from hot smoked trout, slithers of gravad mackerel, pots of marinated rollmops and fillets of smoked eel. Plus there are pots of keta (salmon's eggs) and avruga (herring's eggs). These little balls of fun keep you smiling, whereas if you knew the cruelty involved with some caviar, it would take your appetite away.

Although the Iranian caviar industry seems a better bet than the Russian one – the flavour of the finished product is generally better and the fishermen seem more environmentally aware – most Iranian caviar producers will still throw away the sturgeon fish once their roes are extracted, making it a shockingly wasteful enterprise. With keta and avruga, the eggs taste lovely – and the rest of the fish gets eaten too.

Proper cheeses are not a problem, with lots of traditional British and European varieties at the cheese counter. There are some good slowly-matured Cheddars, including Daylesford's, Keen's and Montgomery's. There's a shockingly rich Gorgonzola, an organic Roquefort papillon, and Colston Basset Stilton, a rich old cheese shot with blue.

Although these cheeses are all high in saturated fats, they're also big on flavour, so a little goes a long way. I thoroughly recommend choosing strongly flavoured, properly matured and high fat cheeses like these over low flavour, low fat, low happy-factor cheeses. You'll find you need to eat a lot less, so they work out better for your figure and better for your pocket, too.

Put some bowls of salad on the table, including something leafy (see page 211 for Leafy Summer Salad), something grainy (try F&W Moroccan Couscous on page 225) and a pulse dish (Kooky Aduki on page 291 is great). People in the Provence region of France know a thing or two about buffet eating and generally lay out a bowl of cold, cooked Puy lentils, drizzled in olive oil and sprinkled with herbes de Provence. Roast your own summer vegetables and serve cold, or stock up on jars of aubergine caviar and aubergine paste, artichoke paste and roasted artichoke hearts, roasted peppers, outrageously esoteric cardoncelli mushrooms, caperberries, pungent marinated garlic cloves and some of the wonderfully different kinds of marinated olives.

Top up the table with fresh mayo, goat's butter, toasted pumpkin seed oil and aged balsamic vinegar and your smörgåsbord is ready – and too delicious for words. Dig in!

DINNER

Pam and Will Best
Manor Farm, Organic Milk Producer, Godmanstone, Dorset

'The quality of our cows' fodder is paramount, so we 'fix' nitrogen naturally by growing alfalfa for silage. We also plant herbs like chicory and salad burnett into the grass for our animals to feed on.'

You've made it. The day is done and you're ready for a well-deserved meal of substantial proportions.

Hungry? So what's on the table?

Some quick meals, some slow meals, some light suppers and some grand feasts – and all of them cooked with the most delicious of ingredients to make eating an unadulterated pleasure.

FUNKY FRIED FISH...

Wild Gilt Head Bream with Shimeji and Tekka

There are lots of different kinds of bream, both freshwater and saltwater, and they're quite different from each other, despite having the same name. Freshwater bream are generally farmed, but not yet organically to my knowledge. Hence I simply don't go there. There are also Australian breams, which are nice, but nothing to do with the local bream that this recipe is for.

There are eight different wild varieties caught in the coastal waters of Europe, from the northern coasts of Norway down to sunny Tenerife. They include tasty black bream and red sea bream, though, to my mind, gilt head bream is the tastiest kind. It's plentiful off the coasts of Wales, Cornwall and France, and can be identified by the little metallic gold spot behind its gills. They're known as *dourades* in France, where they're often lightly fried in a similar way to the method used in this recipe.

Fresh & Wild's gilt head bream are sold whole, so you get to see the gold spot. Once you've picked the one for you, the fishmonger will fillet it for you on request, or leave it whole if you want to do it yourself. Either way, you'll need to get busy with a knife, scraping the scales off the skin under cold running water. Personally, I use my trusty washing-up gloves for this job, as they stop my fingers getting cold and my hands getting smelly. And I use an old paring knife to save my best one from going blunt.

Shimeji mushrooms are a traditional wild variety from Japan, prized for their health-giving properties as well as their flavour and beauty. Fresh & Wild's fresh shimeji are grown by Fundamentally Fungus, a pioneering company founded by Jane Dick. Jane is a microbiologist, a great cook and somebody who is seriously passionate about conservation. As such, her pursuit of gourmet and eco-friendly mushrooms is only natural.

People have been getting into weird and wonderful wild mushrooms in the UK in the last few years, an area of culinary delight previously only really explored in Italy, Germany and France. It's nice that cooks in the UK are waking up to the possibilities around them – but amateur foraging is incredibly destructive environmentally.

We're encouraged to go native, but well-meaning city-dwellers running around the British countryside with plastic bags full of slimly identified fungus just isn't a good idea. We're also offered the easy option, with both fresh and dried wild mushrooms on sale at posh shops throughout the land. But unlike the dried wild mushrooms you'll find in Fresh & Wild, most are sadly lacking verification in terms of the sustainability of the foraging techniques used to gather them.

Mushrooms are delicate things and wild ones support a whole ecosystem of bugs and beasties. According to English Nature, over a thousand species rely on wild fungi in the UK. Pick too many wild fungus on your little foraging trek in the woods and you'll adversely affect loads of tiny creatures.

If it's fresh, wild mushrooms you're after, go for Jane's organically cultivated and superbly flavoured gourmet varieties. They're not wild, they're farmed – but they taste just the same, because they're identical. She's got fresh shiitake and maitake, delicate lilac-stemmed wood blewits, pale gold horse mushrooms and more familiar chestnut mushrooms. And, of course, she also supplies the shimeji that are fried up in this dish, which are beautiful little clusters of slender fairy-style mushrooms, almost too special to eat. But hey, just go for it. That's what they're here for.

Tekka's rich, earthy spiciness is a great addition to the robust fish and the firm-textured shimeji.

It's an ancient condiment made by frying fresh carrots, burdock and lotus roots in sesame oil, and adding hatcho miso paste and minced ginger. The mixture is slowly sautéed for about six hours to make an almost dry, powdery paste. As you can imagine, this stuff's strongly flavoured, so a little goes a long way.

Romanesco cauliflowers are hands down my favourite vegetable by a million zillion miles in terms of appearance. They are simply stunning and elicit gasps of wonder from every single person I've ever shared one with. Their fractal florets curl and twist like some weird sci-fi idea of a vegetable, and they have an otherworldly grace that defies description. Go see for yourself and you'll understand what I mean.

FUNKY F R I E D   F I S H . . .

Wild Gilt Head Bream with Shimeji and Tekka

DINNER FOR 2:

½ a Romanesco cauliflower, carefully cut into florets

1 tablespoon olive oil

2 x 100g fillets of wild gilt head bream, de-scaled and cleaned

100g shimeji, separated into clumps of 3–6 mushrooms

3 garlic cloves, finely crushed

1 heaped teaspoon tekka

½ a lemon, plus lemon quarters for serving

The trick with this dish is to get the pan really hot, then whack the fillets in and out in 5 minutes max. If you have a griddle pan, now is the perfect time to use it, as the charcoal-effect lines on the fish will make it look the business. That said, a normal frying pan will crisp up the skin, too, so you can't go wrong either way.

First, put the cauliflower in a steamer over a saucepan. Pour enough water into the pan to produce a reasonable amount of steam, but not so much that the water touches the steamer as it boils. Place over a medium heat.

Put the oil in the griddle or frying pan, heat until hot, and then add the fish fillets, skin-side down. Add the shimeji and garlic, and fry everything for a couple of minutes. With a fish slice, carefully but quickly lift the fillets and turn them over. With a wooden spatula, mix the shimeji and garlic about, and then sprinkle the tekka onto the mushrooms. Squeeze the lemon juice over them with a sizzle and give the shimeji a good stir.

When the 5 minutes are up, transfer the fish onto plates, and then add the shimeji on the side as soon as they look cooked, i.e. within a minute. Serve with the steamed Romanesco cauliflower, with lemon quarters on the side of each plate for self-squeezing.

BRAISED LEG OF WELSH MOUNTAIN MUTTON

with Roasted Roots

Right up until the Second World War, lamb was scorned as a lesser meat to mutton in terms of both its texture and flavour. Everybody loved the denser texture and the flavour was somehow less sheepy and more gamey. So whatever happened to mutton? Well it disappeared when profit margins became the name of the game. Yep, the accountants stole our mutton.

Confused? Think about it. The most expensive 'ingredient' in most food is time – the time allowed for breads to rise and bake to perfection, the time needed for a cheese to mature to its full flavour and the time needed for a young lamb to enjoy its little life and produce a more flavourful meat when the inevitable visit to the abattoir comes.

Thankfully, Bob and Carolyn Kennard don't seem to have noticed the time thieves. They've been supplying mutton for over a decade from Graig Farm in Radnorshire, Mid Wales. They started off simply trying to raise chickens that tasted of chicken, then expanded to form a network of like-minded farmers. Little by little, they built the Graig Farm Producers Group, a network of around 200 organic farmers committed to 'growing' meat the decent way.

Welsh mountain mutton is the best kind of mutton according to most fans of the meat, including me. This is due to a combination of the wild herbage that's to be found on top of Welsh mountains and the fact that any sheep that manages to survive on such as desolate and difficult terrain has to build up some pretty fine muscle tone. The resilient sheep are at least two years old when they go to meet their makers, which is a ripe old age when compared to the few months that lambs destined for the cheap end of the market get.

I want to make something clear: cheap meat is a bad idea. This isn't because everyone should pay over the odds – everybody shops to a budget and some people's are tighter than other's – but because cheap meat has to be one of the most hideous foodstuffs around. It means cutting corners with your health, and with the length and quality of life for the animal concerned.

I'll come clean – I was vegetarian for about 15 years and vegan for a few of those. The whole idea of eating meat appalled me, but this wasn't because I was squeamish, or because I didn't like the thought of eating animals – and it was certainly nothing to do with not liking the taste. It was all tied up with the horror of the conditions most farm animals endure: the endless doses of antibiotics, the featherless battery chickens with beaks burned to a stub so they can't cannibalize each other, pigs so fat their legs can't hold them up, calves kept in veal crates and fed only liquid to keep their meat pale, cows fed sheep's brains – though I think they've finally learned from that mistake.

However, after a lot of research – and a lot of soul searching – I've worked out that I'm very comfortable about eating organic and biodynamic meat.

Organic meat is raised and slaughtered with respect for the animal. Crimes against animals don't happen on organic farms, and a few organic meat suppliers shine out as particularly noteworthy for the humane way they treat their animals and the traceability of the meat. Graig Farm is one of these.

All Graig Farm mutton has a label on the pack that gives the name of the farmer who raised the sheep and the location of the farm. It also gives the breed of animal and you even see some pictures of the remaining flock, via a web address. All Graig Farm mutton is slaughtered at a small traditional family abattoir up the road, so the sheep enjoy a stress-free time right until the inevitable moment they get the chop. The meat is butchered by hand, with no conveyor belt, and hung to develop an even fuller flavour.

If you don't eat meat because you don't agree with killing animals – or because of the global economics of eating vegetarian food – fair enough. But I'm happy eating decent organic meat that has a proper price tag, reflecting the true cost of a decent life and cruelty-free slaughter. It means I get to eat a balanced quantity of delicious, high-quality, healthy meat – not very often, as it's not an everyday food but a luxury. So, as a treat, bring on the organic mutton, the slow-cooked beef or any of the other organic cruelty-free, fully traceable meats.

And when you're looking for the perfect way to cook that special joint, you can't beat braising, an old-fashioned, slow cooking technique that's dead simple. You'll need a heavy casserole dish with a tight-fitting lid, plus a sheet of greaseproof paper. The idea is to put some chopped veg at the bottom of the pot, put the meat on top of the veg, pour in some liquid, cover with a piece of paper and put the lid on. The veg and liquid will gently give off steam as they cook, adding moisture to the finished cut, which goes meltingly sticky as it slowly braises and also picks up the fresh vegetable flavours. There's a nice exchange going on, with the veg picking up meaty flavours and juices, too, so they cook down to a thick gravy mash.

The fresh bouquet garni is an important element in this recipe. This small bunch of herbs, which is tied together with string, adds a great flavour, but remember to remove it before you serve the dish. It's sort of like bay leaves in a bolognaise, but with company. You can mix and match different combinations, but the mixture I've suggested here is an age-old combination.

The whole dinner does take a long time to cook – that's the nature of slow cooking. But it doesn't take much of your time. The mutton will get on with it unsupervised in the oven, whilst you get on with whatever you want to do. Once everything's in the oven, you've just got to pop into the kitchen for about three minutes once every hour, and bingo – it'll cook itself.

The recipe below features roast parsnips and carrots, but here's another idea for some strange roasted roots. If you can find them (and they are rare), serve this braised mutton dinner with delicious salsify and scorzonera roots roasted on the side. Salsify is a root that looks like a parsnip, but is longer, muddier, thinner and browner. Scorzonera is a kind of salsify, but it has a black skin. Both have a delicate flavour that some people think is like oysters, and a texture a bit like Jerusalem artichokes. When you cut them they release sap, so wash them gently. They'll melt when you roast them, instead of keeping their shape like parsnips and carrots.

BRAISED LEG OF WELSH MOUNTAIN MUTTON

with Roasted Roots

TO MAKE DINNER FOR 4:

25–30cm greaseproof paper

1–2 teaspoons soft butter

100g plain white flour

¼ a nutmeg, grated

2 pinches of pepper

1kg leg of Welsh mountain mutton

2 tablespoons olive oil

2 onions, peeled and sliced

2 sticks celery, chopped into 1cm pieces

1 turnip, chopped into 1cm pieces

A dozen capers

1 bouquet garni of 4 bay leaves, a stem of parsley and a sprig of rosemary

A glass of red wine

Juice of ¼ a lemon

FOR THE ROASTED ROOTS:

300ml sunflower frying oil

2 small carrots or 1 big one, scrubbed, topped and tailed

2 small parsnips or 1 big one, scrubbed, topped and tailed
1 teaspoon dried sage
1 tablespoon tamari
Juice of other ¼ of the lemon

Set the oven to 150°C/300°F/Gas Mark 2. Cut a square of greaseproof paper that is big enough to cover the top of a large casserole dish and leave a bit hanging over the top. Grease the paper with the butter. Mix the flour, nutmeg and pepper in a bowl, then tip the mixture onto the surface.

Cut any majorly gristly bits off the meat and roll the mutton in the flour, coating the whole thing. Heat the oil in a large frying pan, over a high heat, then put the leg in, frying it and turning it with a wooden spoon so that all sides are browned. This shouldn't take more than a few minutes. Take the mutton out of the pan and throw the onions, celery and turnip in. Fry and stir for a few minutes, then take the pan off the heat.

Put the veg, the capers and the bouquet garni into the casserole dish, then pour the glass of wine over them and add the lemon juice. Add hot water until the vegetables are nearly covered. Put the meat on top, then cover the top of the dish with the greased greaseproof paper. Put the lid on and bung the dish in the oven. Come back an hour later and add a bit of hot water to bring the liquid back up to just below the meat. Do the same thing an hour later.

Slice the carrots and parsnips along their lengths, then steam the carrots in a steamer or colander over a covered saucepan of simmering water for about 4 minutes. Add the parsnips and keep steaming. After about 5 minutes check if the roots are cooked; if not steam them for a few more minutes until they're done. Leave them in the colander until later.

Take the mutton out of the oven after 3 hours and, if the liquid has near-ly evaporated, add about 100ml more hot water, and return the dish to the oven. At this point, turn the oven up to 190°C/375°F/Gas Mark 5 and put a roasting tin filled with the oil into the oven. Ten minutes later, add the cooked carrots and parsnips to the roasting tin, and sprinkle over the sage, tamari and lemon juice. Mix everything together well and ensure the veg are coated with liquid, then put the tin back in the oven.

Roast the roots for half an hour, then take them and the braised mutton out of the oven. Carve the leg from the thin end, cutting the meat at a 45-degree angle from the bone. That way you'll get slices that are nice and even. Serve up thick cuts of the meat with the roasted roots and some steamed greens. Drizzle with the cooking juices and thick vegetable gravy mash from the bottom of the dish.

SEITAN AND BURDOCK STIR-FRY

with Buckwheat Soba

Seitan (pronounced *say-tan*) has nothing to do with the devil. No, it's an ancient oriental delicacy used in a similar way to dried tofu. It's made from wheat flour that's been kneaded and rinsed, kneaded and rinsed for absolutely ages, and then simmered in deliciously flavoured liquids like dashi and tamari.

Seitan is very high in protein, but low in fat and carbohydrates.

It's perfectly possible to make seitan at home, but it's a rare person that finds the time these days. Ready-made seitan is completely delicious anyway, so I recommend using the time you've saved to do something more entertaining, like playing loud music and dancing about the living room ...

If possible, use a wok for this recipe. A frying pan will do the job, but the time saved and flavour gained by making a stir-fry in a wok always comes as a shock to those who've never used one before. This is one of those rare occasions when quick is best, as a quick and hot fry means the veg will lose less nutrients, flavour and crunch than when fried in the conventional way. The thin metal and large surface area that makes a wok a wok means maximum heat for quicker, tastier stir-fries.

Burdock is the stuff your grandmother probably gave you at some point in the form of an old-fashioned dandelion and burdock drink. It's the weed with the seed burrs that cover your jumper after a walk through the autumn countryside – the ones with the little hooks that inspired an inventor to dream up Velcro.

The root of the plant is in season during winter, when it's found nestling amongst the pretty carrots like an ugly duckling. It's dark and knobbly and looks as appetizing as sticks, but burdock root soon turns into a swan of a vegetable when scrubbed to reveal its pale and crunchy insides. The taste is subtle and unusual, a bit like water chestnuts and artichokes, and thoroughly delicious. For this reason, I'm convinced it'll soon become way more popular in the UK.

Japanese cooks are very familiar with burdock root, and people on macrobiotic diets will know it too. It's really good for you, with lots of minerals and free-radical fighting phyto-chemicals that give it a reputation as a cancer preventative. But its most eye-opening health benefit is the fact that about a quarter of each burdock root is made up of a substance called inulin, a plant version of insulin. As such, it helps keep your blood sugar levels stable, evening out the rushes and crashes that sugar-sensitive people experience.

Enjoy this stir-fry with traditional Japanese soba noodles. These contain either 40 per cent or 100 per cent buckwheat flour – for this dinner I recommend the 100 per cent variety to balance the seitan.

SEITAN AND BURDOCK STIR-FRY

with Buckwheat Soba

TO FEED 3 PEOPLE:

2 burdock roots, scrubbed

1 tablespoon sunflower oil

1 teaspoon toasted sesame oil

250g soba noodles

2 tablespoons tamari

150g seitan

6 fresh shiitake mushrooms

green nori flakes to sprinkle

Heat a wok or large frying pan over a medium heat. Meanwhile, halve the burdock roots along their lengths and then slice into thin strips. Now add the oils to the pan, then a few seconds later add the slices of burdock. Heating the wok before adding the oil ensures the contents won't stick to it. Fry over a high heat for a few minutes, until the burdock starts to look like it's cooking.

Half fill a large saucepan with boiling water, place on a medium heat, then slide in the noodles. Add the tamari to the wok along with a tablespoon of cold water, so that the burdock root can steam, then throw in the seitan. Turn down the heat a little, cook with the lid on for 5 minutes and then add the mushrooms. Cook for a few more minutes, until the seitan is heated through, the mushrooms are wilted and the burdock looks brown and shiny.

The soba should be ready about the same time. When they are, immediately strain through a colander and rinse under the cold tap. Twirl the soba onto three plates and serve topped with the seitan and burdock root stir-fry. Serve with a bowl of green nori flakes and a bottle of shoyu so people can help themselves.

SAVOURY BREAD AND BUTTER PUDDING

This is a very traditional British dessert recipe that's been turned into a savoury Mediterranean dish. It's comfort food for a rainy day, with perky capers to put the spring back in your step. It's best made with slightly stale bread – in fact, the Victorians invented the original dish for this purpose. Use a light bread for this recipe, as it's one of the occasions when a less dense loaf tastes miles better.

Passata is a great standby for making the world's quickest sauces. It's just chopped, strained tomatoes that are full of flavour. Keep a jar of capers and a tin of sustainably-fished tuna handy, too, ready to transform the barest of ingredients into a delectable meal. Capers are tiny unopened flower buds from a spiny Mediterranean shrub. Other shops often sell them pickled in brine but those stored in olive oil taste better.

Fresh & Wild stock Fish 4 Ever tinned fillets of white and yellow fin tuna, sardines, mackerel, anchovies and herring, all in organic cold-pressed oil. Fish 4 Ever fish not only taste good enough to win a gold award in the annual Great Taste Awards, but they're fished with respect for the marine environment – and the company looks after their fishermen too. They don't serve up endangered species or immature fish, freeze the catch for weeks at sea, process the fish with chemicals or over-cook them. It's just the very freshest and most plentiful kinds of tasty fish served in delicious cold-pressed organic oils.

Tuna is a special treat in my kitchen, whether it's fresh steaks of sustainably-caught yellow fin, or tins of Fish 4 Ever white fin. Tuna fish live in warmer climes than our seas can provide, so the nearest they get to the UK is Spain. That's pretty near compared to hoki fish from New Zealand, but not as short a distance to travel to my hob as the wonderful monkfish, turbot and brill that come from Cornwall.

This recipe features dried wild mushrooms. You'll find these in the bigger stores under the Tropical Wholefoods brand. Dried mushrooms of any kind are intense bundles of flavour that can add heaps of personality to any savoury dish, so keep some in your cupboard at all times. Wild mushrooms on sale in other shops vary wildly in terms of sustainability. Mushrooms are strange and delicate things, with complex ways of reproducing. Thoughtlessly picking wild mushrooms of any kind can damage future supplies dramatically.

Tropical Wholefoods was founded with the number one aim of importing fairly-traded foods from tropical countries, thus providing a way for people to develop good sources of income from their locally-grown foods. As such, their products are sustainable, because the producers cherish their sources and ensure they're nurtured for future generations.

The chanterelles grow wild in a Zambian forest and are collected by women as part of a project run by the Mpongwe Development Corporation. The main activity of Mpongwe is to grow and harvest coffee, but the chanterelles provide essential income for this community when the coffee is off-season. Women from this region are trained to identify, pick and clean the chanterelles with minimum impact to the environment. In fact, by carrying the freshly-picked wild mushrooms in open straw baskets, the women help the natural spore-drifting process. The chanterelles are then dried in the local coffee-roasting centre, ready to be sent off for us to enjoy.

Tropical Wholefoods' porcini mushrooms come primarily from Zimbabwe, although as a highly seasonal product they also import them from Chile and Italy to make sure we can enjoy them all year round. Porcini is the Italian name for these little bundles of flavour. In France they're known as ceps, but my favourite name for them is the old English moniker, honeybuns.

When they've been imported from Zimbabwe, Tropical Wholefoods' porcini come from a huge deciduous forest in a place called Chimanimani, which is right on the border with Mozambique. A wide range of gorgeous and exotic mushrooms grow here, and are collected by cooperatives and dried in the local coffee drying facilities.

Porcini taste rich and smoky, with an intensity that's complimented by strong herbs like thyme. As with all dried mushrooms, 10g of dried mushrooms is the equivalent of 80g of fresh ones. So this is one richly mushroomy pudding ...

SAVOURY BREAD AND BUTTER PUDDING

FOR 4 HELPINGS:

40g dried chanterelles

35g dried porcini

60g butter

8 thick slices of yesterday's light fluffy bread

1 tin yellow-fin tuna

4 garlic cloves, peeled and crushed

700g passata

A handful of flat-leaf parsley, chopped

1 teaspoon dried thyme

1 teaspoon dried oregano

30g capers in olive oil, drained (keep the liquid to use as a vinaigrette)

Generous pinch of coarsely ground pepper

200g buffalo mozzarella, drained and sliced

4 eggs

Wash the mushrooms thoroughly in cold water, then soak them in enough warm water to cover them for about 30 minutes. Turn the oven on to 180°C/350°F/Gas Mark 4. Butter the bread and put half of it into a greased, shallow ovenproof or baking dish, buttered side down. Drain the oil from the tinned fish into a pan, place over a medium heat, add the garlic, and fry, stirring with a wooden spoon. After a minute, add the passata, herbs, capers and pepper, and keep stirring for a few minutes.

Drain the mushrooms (if you want to you can keep the soaking water to use as a liquid seasoning within the following few days). Using kitchen scissors, chop them finely. Flake the tuna, then spread it over the bread. Layer the mushrooms on top of the fish, then put a layer of mozzarella on top.

Crack the eggs into another bowl. Beat them with a fork and then slowly beat in the passata mixture. Pour about two-thirds of the mixture over the pudding. Top the pudding with the rest of the bread, buttered side up, then spread the remaining tomato mixture on top. Bake for about 40–50 minutes. You'll know it's done when it's fairly firm but is still nice and moist in the middle, with a slightly caramelized tomato top.

Take the pudding out of the oven and leave it to rest for about 10 minutes. This'll give the tomato custard time to set a bit more, and let it cool down enough to eat. Serve with steamed florets of purple sprouting broccoli in spring, or standard broccoli the rest of the time. Alternatively, in September and October, you could tantalize your taste buds with new season Brussels sprouts.

FISHY ON A DISHY

My mate Carl is Swedish and lives in London. His mum Diana, being a native of the port of Gothenburg, is the fish queen and cooks a mean mackerel, serving this fishy dishy in summer when mackerel are at their best. These oily fish are great value, strongly flavoured and stuffed full of healthy omega fish oils. They can help protect against heart attacks, arthritis and cardiovascular disease, and can help improve memory, immunity and eye function in children. Mackerel also contain lots of iodine, an essential mineral that helps us to think more clearly. And they're quick to cook – under half an hour from start to finish.

Fresh & Wild's mackerel come fresh from Looe on the Southern Cornish coast. It's a picture-postcard fishing village where things happen the old-fashioned way. Just around the coast, huge international fishing trawlers set out to sea for weeks on end, freezing the catch on-board for a later date. In contrast, Jeffersons Seafoods' fishermen go out from Looe every day in little boats, harvesting their mackerel using hand lines, and deliver the fish fresh to shore every night. Using lines to catch the mackerel ensures you don't get ones that aren't fully grown, as they've got to be mature enough to bite.

These special fish are accompanied by equally special potatoes – blue ones. People in Britain are just starting to get their heads around the concept of floury and waxy potatoes but the entire populations of Peru and Bolivia are conversant with simply hundreds of different kinds.

I travelled to this region a few years ago, staying for a while in the town of Cuzco on the way to Machu Pichu and Lake Titicaca. The big market in the centre of town resembles a culinary festival every single week. Stallholders go to great lengths to supply the most incredibly high quality produce, and create stunning displays from their wares. There are piles of fragrant spices, wooden buckets full of the finest olives I've ever tasted, full-scale artistic displays of beautiful tropical fruits – and one thousand different kinds of potatoes. There are huge ones and tiny ones, white ones and black ones, red ones and green ones, smooth ones and knobbly ones, for Cuzco is the place that all potato varieties hail from.

Fresh & Wild's Edzell blues would be right at home in Cuzco market, but luckily they're cultivated in the UK so we don't have to import them all the way from Peru. And being a waxy variety about the size of Jersey Royals, they're excellent simply boiled or roasted.

Dowsed in kefir, they're gorgeous. This fermented milk product originally comes from the Caucasus Mountains, an area of traditional cuisine encompassing Armenia, Azerbaijan and Georgia. The name loosely translates from Turkish as 'feeling good', which is precisely the effect it has.

Kefir is not the traditional sour cream served in Sweden, but hey ho, I prefer it. It's related to beer as well as to yogurt, thereby combining two great things in one, all within an extremely-good-for-you probiotic context. It also has a light and zesty flavour.

This is a simple dish in terms of preparation and flavours, but the fact that it's not fancy is its strength, delivering fresh, full flavours without the fuss.

FISHY ON A DISHY

4 fresh mackerel on the bone, each about 400g

Sea salt and crushed black pepper

2 fresh lemons, sliced

A bunch of fresh thyme

A bunch of fresh parsley

4 garlic cloves, peeled and sliced

1 kilo Edzell blue potatoes, halved

250g jar of fresh kefir

A handful of fresh chives, chopped

Gut and clean the fish if the fishmonger hasn't already done this. Put the fish in a shallow ovenproof dish. Season with salt and pepper inside and out, then stuff with the lemon slices, herbs and garlic, holding back some herbs to sprinkle on the outside of the fish. Bake in the oven, for about 15 minutes, at 200°C/400°F/Gas Mark 6.

Meanwhile, scrub the potatoes and put them in a saucepan with boiling water to cover and a good pinch of sea salt. Boil for about 15 minutes, or until tender. Drain, then plate along with the mackerel, which should be cooked by now. Pour the kefir over the potatoes and sprinkle with the chopped chives. Serve immediately with salad on the side.

BENARES **TARKA DHAL**

Okay, so this one's a lentil-based soup ... but made properly and served north Indian-style with chapatis, or south Indian-style with plain boiled rice, dhal becomes a dinner. I learned how to make this version on a visit to Benares, also known as Varanassi, or Kashi, the city of Shiva.

Benares is the world's oldest inhabited city and it makes our oldest towns and villages seem like Milton Keynes in comparison. The city is dominated by the River Ganges, with the bustle of the city on one bank and a pristine plain of untouched land on the opposite side. Freshwater dolphins swim in the water, as do many people. Some have come here on their last journey, fulfilling a wish to end their days in such a sacred place. Other people have come to study classical music, as Benares is the most important place in India for sitar and tabla playing. Making music is a spiritual pursuit in Hinduism, so the most sacred city is naturally the centre of musical excellence as well.

The culinary arts are celebrated in this city too, as they are throughout India. Each family has their own unique blend of spices, or garam masalas. Often the spices are grown, roasted and ground in conjunction with different phases of the moon, biodynamically enhancing delicate nuances in the flavours and medicinal properties in the resulting blend. The fragrance of roasting masalas wafts through the narrow streets at mealtimes, and is truly mouthwatering.

This recipe uses split peas along with the compulsory lentils. You'll also need ghee, which most families in India make at home. It's butter that has had the milk protein removed so that it stays fresh for longer. Unlike butter, ghee has a reputation as a healing food that absorbs toxins from the body. It's also an important factor in achieving an authentic flavour. To make it yourself, simply heat some butter gently until the milk solids turn brownish and rise to the surface or fall to the bottom of the pan. Be careful not to let it burn, then either scrape the solids off or strain the liquid through muslin. Allow the fat to solidify as it cools, and there's your ghee. Alternatively, pick up a jar of ready-made organic ghee at Fresh & Wild – you'll find it in the baking section.

Serve this dhal with homemade chapatis (see page 249) and a bowl of brown basmati. And don't worry about the 'best before' date on the rice – in India, rices are kept in the basement to age, a bit like fine wines. You wouldn't say a great quality port from 1960 is out of date, so cherish that bag of basmati at the back of your cupboard!

BENARES **TARKA DHAL**

SERVES 4 PEOPLE:

3 tablespoons ghee

2 medium onions, peeled and finely chopped

2cm piece fresh ginger root, grated

100g red lentils, washed

100g yellow split peas, washed

4 garlic cloves, peeled and finely sliced

2 fresh green chillies, membranes and seeds removed

¼ teaspoon ground white cumin

¼ teaspoon black cumin seeds

¼ teaspoon turmeric

¼ teaspoon ground coriander seeds

¼ teaspoon ground black pepper

2 cardamom pods

2 cloves

2 fresh medium tomatoes, chopped

A handful of fresh coriander, finely chopped

Fresh lemon segments

Heat half the ghee in a large saucepan, over a medium heat, then throw in the onions and ginger when it's hot. Fry for about 6–7 minutes, stirring regularly with a wooden spoon, until the onions are cooked and caramelizing. Add the lentils, split peas and a litre of water, then turn up the heat to

max until it boils. Reduce the heat, cover the pan and leave to simmer, stirring now and then. After about 50 minutes, see if the pulses have completely integrated with the liquid. It should be one big mushy dhal. Remove the
lid, but leave it on the heat.

In a frying pan, heat the rest of the ghee over a medium heat and then
add the garlic, chillies and dried spices. Stir thoroughly for a minute or so
to roast them, releasing their exquisite aromas. Add the tomatoes and their
juice, which will sizzle. Keep stirring and cooking for about 5 minutes, or
until everything looks deliciously cooked. Turn the heat off both pans, then
pour the spices into the lentils and mix well. Serve with the lemon segments on the side, so everyone can add their own squirt of juice. And
watch out for the cardamom pods and cloves, which aren't meant to be
swallowed (though they won't cause any harm if they are).

EASY AS PIE – FRAGRANT DUCK AND CHANTERELLE PIE

with a Sweet Potato Lid

There are two kinds of savoury pies – those made with a pastry crust and those made with a mashed potato lid. I've called this mashed potato pie easy, not because pastry is at all difficult to make, but because mashed potato is even easier.

This particularly easy-as-pie pie features the classic marriage of flavours that is duck, red wine, citrus and sweet potatoes. It's a sticky, heady mix that's pleased people's taste buds for aeons, with a slightly medieval whimsy about it.

If you fancy making an almost-as-easy pie, simply substitute a short-crust pastry lid for the mashed sweet potato. You'll need 200g flour, 100g butter or marg and 2 tablespoons of water to make enough for this entirely un-traditional filling.

Fresh & Wild only sell wild duck meat when it's in season. Any of the cuts will do – leftover leg meat will be just as delicious as prime breast. You can use organic chicken the rest of the year, but cut down the cooking time by 10 minutes. Alternatively, use organic red meats like beef or lamb, and cook the pie for about 20 minutes longer.

EASY AS PIE – FRAGRANT DUCK AND CHANTERELLE PIE

with a Sweet Potato Lid

TO MAKE AN EASY PIE FOR 4 PEOPLE:

10g dried chanterelles

1 kg Joubere (or 1 litre homemade) warm chicken stock

250g dried Puy lentils or brown lentils

5cm piece of dried kombu

500g duck meat, chopped into chunks

1 orange, squeezed for juice and zest shredded

1 tablespoon wholemeal flour

10g kuzu, ground in a suribachi or powdered on the back of a spoon

4 teaspoons dried Quatre Epice spice blend

2 tablespoons olive oil

2 big onions, peeled and chopped

1 big carrot, scrubbed and diced

2 sticks celery, strings removed and finely chopped

1 big beefy tomato, finely chopped

A glass of red wine

1 teaspoon dried thyme

2 bay leaves

250g swede, scrubbed and diced
500g sweet potatoes, scrubbed and diced
A big knob of butter
A drop of whole milk

Wash the chanterelles in cold water, then add to the stock and leave to soak. Boil the lentils and the kombu in 750ml of water for about 45 minutes. Put the chopped duck into a bowl, sprinkle the orange zest onto it and pour the orange juice over the top. Mix the flour, kuzu and spices on a plate, throw the flour mixture over the meat and turn the chunks in the powder so that it's covered and gooey. Leave to marinate in the fridge while the lentils cook and the chanterelles soak. When the lentils are cooked soft, start the next part of this recipe.

In a deep frying pan or a large saucepan, heat the oil over a medium heat. When it's hot, add the onions, carrot and celery. Stir everything with a wooden spatula for a couple of minutes and then add the tomato. Cook for a minute, stirring. Add the duck and the marinade to the pan, and fry so everything sizzles for a couple of minutes. Add the wine and the herbs, and stir so that the marinade combines nicely with the liquid. Pour in the stock, making sure the mushrooms don't fall in, then throw in the lentils. Wait for everything to heat up to a boil, then turn the heat down low, cover the pan and simmer for an hour. Stir in the chanterelles, then cover and continue to sauté.

At this point, put the swede into a pan of boiling water over a medium heat. Keep boiling for about 10 minutes, then add the sweet potato. Cover the pan and turn the heat down so that it simmers. Turn the oven on to 190°/375°F Gas Mark 5. After 10 more minutes, check if the swede and potatoes are soft yet and keep boiling if they're not. You want them soft enough to mash easily, otherwise it's not 'easy' pie. When the veg is very soft, drain the water off carefully, add the butter and milk to the saucepan and mash away with a big masher.

At this point, the pie filling will smell divine. Whip it off the heat, pick out the bay leaves with a fork and ladle it into a shallow ovenproof dish. Spoon the mash on top and either shape it into peaks or use a fork to make a pattern such as flowers or a stylish checker board – or how about adding your initial, just like they did in medieval days. Anyway, once you've got all those arts and crafts feelings properly expressed, bung the pie in the oven on top of a baking sheet (to catch any gravy that might boil over).

Come back in half an hour and serve the pie with lightly steamed cabbage or mustard greens, or a lovely fresh leafy salad.

ROMANTIC **CORNISH GURNARD**

on a Rice Noodle Pillow

I love the fact that Fresh & Wild fish and seafood counters are full of species that you've never come across before, or fish that you do know, but not quite in the form you see before you. Fish like monkfish and black cod, which are firm in texture and sweet in flavour. Big whole cod, sustainably fished, but still unbelievably ugly. And old favourites like John Dory, Gilt Head bream and clams, all impeccable and delicious.

My love of unusual seafood isn't just a foodie thing, although the discovery of new taste sensations is wonderful. The main reason less familiar varieties are so exciting is that by finding different types of fish and seafood to enjoy, the pressure is taken off species that are in danger of extinction. The fact that everyone loves cod and chips means there's not enough sustainably-sourced cod to satisfy demand. Rather than going without fish at all, choosing a more unusual variety opens up your horizons whilst ensuring over-fished species get a chance to survive our voracious appetites. And remember, local is best both for freshness and for sustainability.

This is a special fish, so treat it with the respect it deserves by giving it a serious marinade. Cornish gurnard has a very firm white flesh and a delicate flavour, so it can more than hold its own with this rich, sweet miso marinade. The miso flavours the firm flesh whilst the mirin tenderizes it.

This dish is great for a romantic meal – after all you have to be pretty sweet on somebody to splash out on these classy fillets and marinate them for two days before the special night. And to make the dish even more special, the fish is presented on a pillow of translucent rice noodles. Cornish Thai cuisine ... delicious!

ROMANTIC **CORNISH GURNARD**

on a Rice Noodle Pillow

DINNER FOR 2:

125g sweet white miso
75ml mirin
2 x 200g fillets of Cornish gurnard
125g organic Thai rice noodles
1 teaspoon toasted sesame oil

Put the miso into a medium-sized ovenproof dish and mix in the mirin. Put the fish in and massage the miso mixture into the flesh. Make sure that the fillets are completely covered in the paste, then put the oven dish into a plastic carrier bag and then in your fridge. Two days later, turn your oven on to 200°C/400°F/Gas Mark 6. Wait for 10 minutes before you cook the fish. During this time, don a pair of clean washing-up gloves and take the fish dish out of the fridge. Pick up each fillet, scrape the miso mixture off the fish and discard it. Put the clean fish onto a plate, wash the ovenproof dish, then put the fillets back into it. Bake the fish in the oven for 15 minutes.

When the fish is almost cooked, plunge the noodles into a big saucepan of boiling water. Add the oil to the pan and keep the heat on so that the water boils again. Boil the noodles for 3 minutes, drain them in a colander and then rinse in boiling water.

Twirl the noodles onto each plate, then take the gurnard fillets out of the oven and carefully place each one onto its pillow using a fish slice. Serve with a sea vegetable salad (see page 222), assorted sushi pickles and cups of sake.

SLOW BEEF, NAMEKO AND APRICOT STEW

with Jerusalem Artichokes

One of the joys of living in a city full of different culinary traditions is mixing and matching bits and bobs from all over the world. There's inspiration in this dish from Scandinavia, the Middle East and Japan – and why not! This dinner is truly delicious when enjoyed with Jerusalem artichokes, which are in season during autumn. Later into winter, adapt the recipe by using other delicately flavoured vegetables, such as kohlrabi.

Organic beef is so much better for your health than beef from most cows that, strangely enough, don't eat grass. Instead, most non-organic cows are given dried food preparations, as they are often kept inside barns all year round, hardly ever walking about in open fields. Unsurprisingly, they're also routinely fed various growth-promoting hormones and antibiotics. And while we're on the topic of cows, if you cook with veal, it's essential it's organic. Organic veal is simply meat from young cows that have been nursed on their mother's milk, and is a by-product of the organic dairy industry. Organic dairy cows need to give birth to calves about once a year to keep them producing milk, and the male calves end up as organic veal after they're suckled. Non-organic veal, in contrast, is the meat of young male calves which have been stuck in a veal crate and force-fed milk to make their flesh pale. Disgusting. By eating organic veal, you are making sure that young calves are neither raised in cruel continental veal crates, nor simply slaughtered at birth and thrown away. Organic veal is reassuringly darker in colour than the standard stuff, a further assurance that the calves have been raised humanely with a varied diet. It's also more developed in terms of flavour and texture.

Organic beef is a lot leaner than non-organic beef, with the fat less marbled into the meat, making it easier to cut away. And it's way better on the cholesterol front too, with a much healthier balance of good and bad cholesterol. All organic red meats contain a powerful antioxidant called L-Carnitine, which helps wounds to heal quicker and improves your skin tone. It's also thought to help protect the brain from Alzheimer's disease, and it can help prevent cataracts.

Health aside, organic beef, veal and all other organic meats are just so much tastier than their non-organic equivalents. The animals have been walking about happily doing what they do, so the meat is invariably meatier and less fatty. And organic farmers generally breed specialist and heirloom breeds, animals that they are committed to, and they are farmed for flavour instead of simply for the size of their rumps. In addition, good quality organic meat is properly hung and cured and generally made as tasty as can be.

Fresh & Wild stocks beef from Wootton Organic, an amazing 4500-acre farm in Derbyshire, run by Lady Bamford. The cows, deer and sheep live out their entire life cycle on the farm. Almost all other meat-rearing farms have to send their animals out to be slaughtered, whereas Wootton Organic animals are conceived, born, raised and eventually slaughtered all within the farm, which is in an area of outstanding natural beauty.

Almost all other meat animals are bred through artificial insemination, but Wootton cattle need no encouragement or syringes to get busy in the romance department. Their happy, stress-free lives in blissful surroundings provide the perfect backdrop to natural mating. And at the other end of the life cycle, about three months before it's time for them to become steaks, the animals are gently moved to the field nearest the on-site abattoir. This means there's no stress from transportation in cramped lorries and, importantly, the animals don't get to see each other get the chop. This humane treatment makes their lives and deaths more dignified and it means their meat is untarnished by the stress hormones present in meat from stressed beasts.

The fresh nameko mushrooms in this recipe come from Fundamentally Fungus, a pioneering organic company based near Winchester. These little amber-coloured Japanese mushrooms have a sticky, jelly-like texture and earthy flavour that's a perfect counterfoil to slow-stewed beef. You'll find them in stylish packs in the fresh produce section, alongside the other fresh cultivated mushrooms.

The ajowan seed is a lesser-known ingredient from Parsee and Gujarati cuisine. It's an excellent ingredient for reducing the sort of windiness caused by artichoke and pulse dishes. The seeds have got a really strong thyme flavour, almost like thyme crossed with tea tree oil, and this complements the buttery artichoke flavours really nicely.

SLOW BEEF, NAMEKO AND APRICOT STEW

with Jerusalem Artichokes

DINNER FOR 6:

600g beef stock (2 pots of Joubere)

A glass of red or white wine

2 tablespoons tamari

200g dried hunza apricots

1kg beef stewing steak or rump steak

2 tablespoons plain wholemeal flour

4 tablespoons olive oil

1 teaspoon ground coriander

1 teaspoon ground pepper

1 fresh red chilli, deseeded and coarsely chopped

6 garlic cloves, peeled

200g fresh nameko or chestnut mushrooms, halved

A few sprigs of marjoram or 1 teaspoon dried marjoram

A handful of fresh sage or 1 teaspoon dried sage

ARTICHOKES:

6 teaspoons ajowan seeds

1kg Jerusalem artichokes, scrubbed

1 tablespoon sunflower oil
2 tablespoons olive oil
6 shallots, peeled and coarsely chopped
A good pinch of sea salt

The night before, mix the beef stock, wine and tamari, add the apricots and leave to soak. Next day, pit the hunzas, keeping the stones as well as the apricot halves. Reserve the marinade.

Heat the oven to 160°C/325°F/Gas Mark 3, then cut the beef into cubes of 2–3cm. Put the flour onto a plate and roll the meat in it to coat the chunks. In a large frying pan, heat the 4 tablespoons of olive oil over a medium heat. Add the dried spices, fresh chilli and whole cloves of garlic. Fry until they start to smell good, about 1 minute, stirring constantly with a flat wooden spatula. Throw in the beef, brown it for a few minutes, then add the mushrooms and fry for a further few minutes.

Tip the contents of the pan into a casserole or tagine dish and throw in the marjoram and sage. Pour the apricot soaking liquid into the frying pan, swish around all the browned cooking fats and flavours, then pour into the casserole dish, scraping any solid tasty bits in with the wooden spatula. Throw in the apricots then, with a pair of nut crackers, crack the stones. Pick out the little almond-like nuts and add them to the stew. Cover and cook the stew for about 1½ hours.

When the stew is nearly cooked, grind the ajowan seeds with a suribachi and surikogi, or a pestle and mortar. If you don't have either of these, put the seeds in a plastic bag, make sure there's no air in it, and bash with a rolling pin to bruise the husks. Chop the big artichokes in half so that all the pieces are a similar size, and gouge out any artichoke eyes or dodgy bits.

Heat the sunflower oil and the 2 tablespoons of olive oil in the frying pan over a medium heat. Throw in the ground ajowan and shallots, and stir with the spatula. About a minute later, add the artichokes and keep stirring for a couple of minutes. Pour in 75ml of hot water, cover the pan and simmer over a low to medium heat for about 10 minutes. Take the lid off and turn the heat up, boiling off the liquid for about 5 minutes.

Take the stew out of the oven and serve up with the artichokes on the side.

OCTOPUS STEW

It seems people either love octopus or hate it. My boyfriend can't eat enough of them. He could eat octopus for England, especially when cooked with his other great love, red wine. If the thought of eating all those tentacles leaves you cold, just try it out – you may discover you're missing out on something lovely. After all, most of the Mediterranean is hooked.

Proper, fully-grown octopuses are fiendishly difficult to find in the UK. So hard to find, in fact, that, until recently, a friend of a friend used to bring frozen tentacles back from Cyprus every year in his hand luggage. Such are the lengths that octopus fans will go to.

However, fear not. Octopus is sold at Fresh & Wild's fresh fish counters. The brilliant thing about the fresh fish counters – other than the octopuses and assorted sea beasties – are the fishmongers. They're passionate about fish and seafood, know which fish is best on that day and what's so great about each variety. In fact, they can't wait to help you choose your dinner.

And when it comes to octopuses, Fresh & Wild's fishmongers are dead handy, as they'll prepare it for you, cutting off the tentacles, removing the ink and getting rid of any particularly otherworldly bits of the beast. They're highly skilled people, many of whom have worked in the kitchens of some top restaurants, which is good to know, as most of us are likely to make a pig's ear of an octopus's tentacle.

OCTOPUS STEW

DINNER FOR 4:

1kg octopus, prepared by your friendly Fresh & Wild fishmonger

4 red onions, peeled and sliced

4 tablespoons olive oil

6 garlic cloves, peeled and crushed

A pinch of crushed black pepper

A pinch of ground mace

4 bay leaves

1 teaspoon dried oregano

1 teaspoon dried rosemary

1 teaspoon dried thyme

4 medium tomatoes, chopped

2 tablespoons red wine vinegar

A glass of red wine

A handful of flat-leaf parsley, finely chopped

Put the octopus and about a quarter of the chopped onion into a medium saucepan over a low heat. Cover with hot water from the kettle, put the lid on and simmer for about an hour.

Drain the octopus and onion through a colander into a bowl. Keep the water for another time – use it as a stock for a soup. Discard the onion and the octopus head, and chop the rest of the beastie into chunks. Heat the oil in a large saucepan over a medium heat and, when it's hot, throw in the octopus, garlic and the rest of the onions. Fry and stir with a wooden spoon, turning the chunks so that everything fries evenly. When the onions begin to go brown, add the spices and dried herbs and fry for another minute or so. Now add the tomatoes, vinegar and wine, and heat on high until the liquid is bubbling.

Put the lid on the pan and turn the heat right down, as low as it will go without going out. Leave the stew to simmer for about an hour and a half. Don't look at it too often, as every time you peek, you'll lose some heat. Finally, succumb to the potent, rich smells emanating from your kitchen. Ladle the stew into bowls, sprinkle over some parsley and serve with buttered Boozy Beer Bread (see page 248) or pitta bread.

TOFU, WAKAME AND LOTUS
ROOT STIR-FRY

Tofu is a really versatile ingredient. I've used it here marinated, as its bland flavour is the perfect canvas for strong combinations of tastes. However, it's just as at home picking up sweet tones, as it does in the Orange, Almond and Brandy Tarts recipe on page 175 or the Cherry Chocolate Spread on page 275.

Everybody knows that tofu is good for you, but it's particularly good for women. In Japan, no word exists for hot flushes, and scientists believe that the reason Japanese women don't suffer from them is because of the high amounts of tofu and soy milk in the Japanese diet. These foods are rich in the natural phyto-chemicals that help balance unruly hormones. The traditional Japanese diet also doesn't contain dairy milk. This is believed to be a major reason why this island nation didn't get osteoporosis or breast cancer at Western levels until recently – basically since they started eating more Western foods.

Wakame is one of the sea vegetables I use most regularly, and its mild flavour makes it a useful starter sea veg. It's good either soaked and eaten as a salad or chopped and added to hot dishes. You can also add a bit to bean and pulse dishes to make them less windy. Alternatively, make a sprinkle – heat your oven 150°C/300°F/Gas Mark 2, put some dried wakame in, turn off the oven and leave the wakame in there for half an hour. You can then crumble it into a powder that can be added to food in the kitchen or at the table, instead of salt.

Lotus root is one of the prettiest vegetables you could wish to come across. Its Swiss cheese-sized holes run through the length of the vegetable, which is a sort of underwater buoyancy stem for the lotus flower. It's said to be good for your lungs and for raising general energy levels, and is sold in Fresh & Wild sliced and dried.

TOFU, WAKAME AND LOTUS ROOT STIR-FRY

FOR 4 PEOPLE:

50g dried lotus root

4 tablespoons tamari

1 teaspoon cider vinegar

1 tablespoon mirin

4cm piece fresh ginger root, grated

4 garlic cloves, peeled and crushed

175g tofu

40g wakame

2 medium carrots, scrubbed, topped and tailed

1 tablespoon toasted sesame oil

2 tablespoons sunflower oil

2 tablespoons sesame seeds

TAMARI RICE:

200g short-grain brown rice

750ml water

2–4 tablespoons tamari, to taste

1 tablespoon sesame seeds

Submerge the lotus root in warm water. On a plate, mix the tamari with the vinegar, mirin, ginger and garlic. Slice the tofu and spread it onto the plate, turning it to cover it in the marinade. Leave the tofu and the lotus root for 2 hours, covering if you have a cat or inquisitive kids.

About an hour and a half after you've set aside the tofu and lotus root, make the tamari rice. Put the rice in a large pan with the cold water. If you like your rice darkly sticky with salty tamari, use lots of tamari, but if you just want a subtle richness, add less. Either way, add tamari to taste, then heat on high until the water boils. Put the lid on and turn the heat down so it simmers. Leave the rice to cook, checking every now and then that it's not running dry.

Twenty minutes later, break up the wakame with your hands into 2–4cm pieces, then submerge it in warm water to cover. Slice the carrots thinly, and heat the oils in a wok or frying pan over a medium heat. When it's hot, throw in the carrots and sesame seeds, cover and reduce the heat to low. Cook for a few minutes, stirring with a wooden spoon now and then. Turn the heat back up to medium, uncover and add the tofu with its marinade.

Fish the lotus root slices out of their soaking water, keeping the liquid. Chop the lotus into bite-sized chunks, then throw the root into the wok or pan. Fish out the wakame, shake off the excess water, and do the same. Stir everything about. If the mixture looks dry, add some of the wakame or lotus root soaking water by the tablespoonful.

Take everything off the heat and serve up, with separate bowls for the tamari rice and the stir-fry.

VEGETARIAN HAGGIS

with Neeps, Tatties and Whisky Sauce

There always seems to be an air of comedy about haggis that I can't quite fathom out. Is it the word? The vague suspicion that it's made from sheep's eyes and cow's bottoms? I don't know the answer, but I do know that every southerner should give it a go.

The real deal is made from a sheep's stomach stuffed with its heart and liver, some finely minced beef suet, a handful of oats, diced onion, gravy and flavourings, and a twist of lemon. Vegetarian haggis isn't. It's basically an oaty nut roast with added lentils and kidney beans – and lots of Scottish herbs.

Fresh & Wild stock a vegetarian haggis from master haggis makers MacSween's of Edinburgh. Good haggis makes great eating – try it the time-honoured way with tatties, neeps and a wee dram of whisky sauce.

VEGETARIAN HAGGIS

with Neeps, Tatties and Whisky Sauce

FEEDS 2 PEOPLE:

1 vegetarian haggis

2 jacket potato-sized Maris Piper potatoes, or another floury variety

¼ a big swede

284ml carton single cream

50ml semi-skimmed milk

1 egg

A big knob of butter

FOR THE SAUCE:

A knob of butter

2 shallots, finely chopped

10g kuzu root

250g Joubere (or 250ml homemade) vegetable stock

1 tablespoon wholegrain mustard

A dash of whisky

Cut the haggis out of the plastic wrapper and wrap it in a generous layer of foil. Make sure you turn both ends of the foil up before scrunching to seal the parcel. Place in a casserole dish, add about 3cm of cold water and bake in the oven at 180°C/350°F/Gas Mark 4. It will take about 45 minutes to heat right through.

About 20 minutes before the haggis is ready, peel and then chop the potatoes and swede into cubes of about 3–4cm. Put the potatoes and swede into separate saucepans, covering both in boiling water. Heat both pans so the water boils.

Melt the knob of butter for the sauce in a frying pan, add the shallots and powdered kuzu and fry on a medium heat until the shallots go translucent. Squash the kuzu lumps in a saucer with the back of a metal spoon, then throw the kuzu powder in and stir with a wooden spoon. Now add the stock. Stir in the mustard and whisky with a fork and simmer.

Remove the potatoes from the heat after about 8–10 minutes and drain thoroughly. Pour the cream and milk into a bowl, then whisk the egg in with a fork. Pour this cream mixture into the potato pan, then heat it until it's simmering. Keep cooking until the potatoes are soft, about 5 minutes. Remove both the potatoes and the swede from the heat, and drain the swede thoroughly. Add the butter to the swede and then mash both the swede and potatoes.

Serve half a haggis for each person with separate mounds of neeps (swede) and tatties, smothered in the whisky sauce – perfect for a cold winter's evening.

NUT RICE NOT RISOTTO

Call me strange, but I don't like risotto. All that soggy, gooey white rice makes me want to skip straight to pudding. And before you point out the rice pudding recipe in this very book, please note that sweet, soggy, gooey rice is a completely different thing.

So what's a girl to do when she's been running on empty all day and needs some delicious stodge *right now?*

Enter this wondrous rice dish made with last night's leftovers. After all, it seems to be impossible to boil rice without making too much. I've suggested a great tasting combination of veg in this recipe, but feel free to use any other mix that happens to be in the fridge. Avoid roots and tubers, other than carrots, but most things that grow above ground work very nicely if cooked in order, from the hardest to the softest varieties.

You may notice there are three cloves of garlic for this one-portion recipe – well why not? You can push the boat out seeing as you're eating on your own. Go on, have some fun followed by a long hot soak in the bath ...

NUT RICE NOT RISOTTO

DINNER FOR 1:

1 tablespoon olive oil

1 tablespoon sesame oil

1 small onion, peeled, halved and finely sliced

A little white, red or green cabbage, finely shredded

3 garlic cloves, peeled and crushed

⅓ of an aubergine, finely chopped

¼ a courgette, halved lengthwise and sliced into half moons

A pinch of nutmeg

150g yesterday's cooked, short-grain brown rice

1 teaspoon herbes de Provence

A handful of walnut pieces, crushed

6 fat caperberries, stalks removed and berries chopped

Heat the oils in a large frying pan or a wok over a medium heat. When they're hot, add the onion and cabbage. Stir about with a wooden spatula for a minute or two and then throw in the garlic, aubergine, courgette and nutmeg. Let that lot sizzle for a couple of minutes until the veg look nearly cooked.

Add the rice, herbs, walnuts and caperberries, plus a tablespoon of water. Turn the heat down and put a lid on the pan. The trick is to heat up the rice without it burning and sticking to the pan. And, impatient as we are, the only way to do this is by cooking the covered pan over a gentle low heat, stirring every now and then with your spatula. Anytime it looks like things are getting a bit crisp, add another tablespoon of water and put the lid back on to steam cook.

From start to finish, this dish will take 15 minutes max – it's ready when the rice is thoroughly heated. Serve with a bottle of tamari, a jar of tomato ketchup and a pot of mayo on the table alongside the salt and pepper.

PS I take it all back, when a risotto is slow-cooked with proper vialone nano risotto rice, and lavish ingredients like morels, anchovies and saffron ...

SWEET THINGS

Women from the Mango So business in Toussiana, Burkina Fasa, West Africa, gathering ripe mangoes to be peeled, cut, laid on trays and dried.

Mango So is a member of the co-operative Cercle des Secheurs which supplies dried organic mangoes to Tropical Wholefoods, a fair trade supplier to Fresh & Wild.

I want to have my cake and eat it.

We've been good and deserve nice sweet things – but nothing full of refined sugar or smothered in hideous icing sugar, thanks very much.

Here's a whole bunch of original ideas for sweet things that are more fun. They're properly sweet, with not a grain of refined sugar in sight.

Tuck in, anything's possible.

APPLE AND CHESTNUT TEMPURA

with Sticky Ginger Sauce

Japanese kitchens sizzle with the sound of savoury tempura being deep-fried. A thin ice-cold batter is used to coat little chunks of vegetables, seafood and fish, which are then plunged into very hot oil for only a couple of minutes before being whisked out and served with a soy, mirin and dashi dipping sauce and sushi pickles on the side.

So why not do the same thing with fruit and serve it with a sweet dipping sauce? Here's my recipe for a tempura dessert made from apples and chestnut flour. It's very quick and easy, tastes delicious and preserves almost all the nutrition of the fruit whilst making them a more attractive bet for the non-fruit-eaters in your life.

I suggest using Clearspring sunflower oil for frying. It's cold pressed from a kind of sunflower seed that is naturally 2–3 times higher in monounsaturated oleic acid than most sunflower seeds. That means it is one of the few oils that's suitable for deep-frying whilst being unrefined and full of nutrition.

Clearspring's malt syrups are brilliant too, as they're really sweet and sticky but don't give you a sugar rush or a sugar crash like other syrups.

The brown rice and chestnut flours featured in this recipe add so much texture and flavour that you absolutely must use them – don't be tempted to substitute boring wheat flour. Chestnut flour is sweet, almost cinnamony. It's one of the most delicious kinds of flour in the galaxy, but it's so underused in the UK, it's a scandal. And it's not that it's an old-fashioned ingredient that's been forgotten. No, it's an ingredient that seems to have always been embraced on the continent and disgraced over here.

Sweet chestnuts were introduced to Britain by the Romans – the same people who brought us **wine and wheat**.

Although we went for these other edibles like there's no tomorrow, we primarily fed the chestnuts to our pigs. In Italy, they've developed hundreds of different uses for chestnut flour, including a truly delicious porridge-like polenta. And in Corsica, you simply can't get married without serving up stacks and stacks of delicacies made out of chestnut flour – twenty-two, to be precise.

Once the packet is open, use up the flour within four months, or the sweet flavour will go weirdly bitter. You shouldn't have a problem slipping a bit into lots of sweet or savoury dishes, from meat stews to delicate fairy cakes. Chestnut flour has probably the highest amount of vitamin C of any kind of flour, so it's good to use it in recipes that don't need to be cooked. That said, it's a much more thickening kind of powder than normal wheat flour, so use it to make béchamel-style sauces, or to thicken up soups or tempura batter.

APPLE AND CHESTNUT TEMPURA

with Sticky Ginger Sauce

TO MAKE 4 PORTIONS OF APPLE AND CHESTNUT TEMPURA:

75g brown rice flour

1kg firm eating apples, such as Jonagold or Laxton's Superb

1 litre bottle of cold-pressed frying sunflower oil

1 tablespoon toasted sesame oil

20g kuzu, ground in a suribachi or powdered on the back of a spoon

75g chestnut flour

300ml iced fizzy mineral water

FOR THE SWEET SAUCE:

3cm piece fresh ginger root

100ml brown rice malt syrup

Put 25g of the rice flour into a shallow dish or plate. Quarter and core the apples, then slice each quarter of an apple into three even-sized wedges. Toss each wedge of apple into the rice flour, and then cover the pieces to stop them going brown too quickly.

Grate the ginger root finely, using a traditional Japanese ceramic ginger grater, a suribachi or a very sharp fine steel grater. Squeeze the grated ginger pulp over a small pan to collect the juice, then add 100ml of boiling water and the malt syrup. Heat the mixture over a low heat until the ingredients blend together. Bring the sauce to a gentle simmer, still over a low heat, stirring every now and then to keep it from boiling. Be careful that the sauce doesn't boil or burn.

Pour the oil into another small saucepan and heat, ready to deep-fry the apples. Be careful not to heat the oil too much, as the aim is to keep it just hot enough to deep-fry, but not so hot that it loses its flavour and gets dangerous.

Throw the kuzu, the rest of the rice flour and all of the chestnut flour into a bowl with the ice-cold water. Mix with a fork, but don't squash out the lumps, as they'll be nice when they go crispy.

When the oil is hot enough for deep-frying and the batter has just been mixed and is still ice cold, dunk each apple piece into the batter, then put it straight into the oil, using a slotted spoon. Fish the apple tempura out after about 2 minutes and place on kitchen paper. Repeat this process for all the apple wedges. Remove the sauce from the heat and serve the apple tempura on individual plates drenched with sticky ginger sauce.

VACHERIN MONT D'OR

with Fresh Pears and Figs

Vacherin Mont d'Or is a hand-crafted cheese from the Swiss Alps. It's exactly the same as a French Alpine cheese Vacherin du Haut-Doubs, but because of some legislative twist of fate the French version has a different name. The French actually invented it, but whichever version you buy, it's round, with a white-speckled pinkish velvety crust that you can't eat, and whose gentle folds and ripples hold back the fragrant creamy cheese inside.

The cheeses are about 12cm wide and 6cm deep and come in a round spruce box that helps to flavour the cheese. Like many Alpine cheeses, it's seasonal, arriving in the shops at the end of September and disappearing again in March. That's because it's made from spring milk that's been maturing all summer ready for the long, cold Alpine winters.

If you're determined to try this delectable and genuinely luscious cheese, pre-order it from Fresh & Wild before it comes into season, as it's very popular with anyone who's tried it before. You can eat Vacherin Mont d'Or at room temperature if you want, and very nice it is too, but it's by heating it that you'll transform the cheese from a tasty creaminess to its full-flavoured and uniquely liquid state. Served hot, it's kind of like a fondue without the Seventies vibe. And it makes a great gift, too, so good that it made my friend Vanessa weep with happiness. Not every cheese can do that …

VACHERIN MONT D'OR

with Fresh Pears and Figs

TO SERVE 6 PORTIONS:

1 Vacherin Mont d'Or cheese

3 Anjou pears

3 figs

Some oatcakes, water biscuits and Dr Karg's crackers

Take the plastic wrapping off the cheese and put it back into its wooden box with the lid on top. Put the box onto a baking tray and heat in an oven set to 150°C/300°F/Gas Mark 2. While the cheese is baking, peel the pears and slice the figs. Cut them each in half lengthways, then pull or cut out the stems and cores. Slice thinly lengthways.

Take the cheese out of the oven after 10–15 minutes. Spread the fruit slices and crackers around the cheese on a platter, then pierce the crust and pull it back to reveal the liquid inside. Serve with lots of spoons and plates so everyone can help themselves. It's gooey, simple and delicious.

CHOCOLATE TAGLIATELLE

with Strawberry Sauce

You may think there's absolutely no reason on earth why anyone with a life should make pasta from scratch. From a taste and texture point of view, there are loads of perfectly brilliant pastas out there, organic or otherwise. Of course, it's good to be sure that the eggs in your ready-made pasta are at the very least free range, but buying organic pasta will guarantee that. Homemade pasta does taste better than any shop-bought ones, but unless you've got oodles of time on your hands, you'll need to find a fantastic excuse to justify the generous amount of time it takes to make.

So here's your excuse – sweet pasta, like chocolate, orange or cinnamon. Trust me. I've made it and it's worth it.

To my knowledge, you simply can't find this sort of sweet pasta ready-made and hey, making pasta at home is a really relaxing and enjoyable way to spend a weekend afternoon.

If you want to try your hand at this dish, you'll need to invest about thirty quid in a pasta-rolling machine. It's like an old-fashioned clothes mangle, but wee, with different cutting attachments for spaghetti and tagliatelle thrown in as standard. Pasta dough is much harder and more resilient than pastry and there's no way you can roll it flat without the widget, so start saving or hinting if you yearn for chocolate pasta.

There's a lot of old rubbish talked about which flours are best for pasta making. Generally, style magazines and colour supplements seem to suggest using '00' flour. However, Italian cooks use flour made from durum wheat. They say that superfine '00' ordinary wheat flour is best used for homemade puff pastry and other very light dishes, such as sponge cakes, and that '0' flours are not as finely milled, so are better for pasta doughs. Personally, I'll take their word for it. Durum wheat is a much harder and higher protein grain than standard wheat, so the dough that's made from its flour is firmer and more elastic. The higher protein levels give the rolled out pasta dough good stretching powers, so you can roll it thinner without it tearing.

Dove's Farm makes a '0' blend that's a mixture of ordinary wheat flour and durum wheat flour, and it's the best organic pasta flour I've found so far. Pasta dough made with Dove's has a lot of stretchiness and keeps its shape when boiled, no problemo. The more durum wheat the better seems to be the general Italian rule of thumb, so give Dove's Farm a bit of encouragement by buying this product. That way maybe, just maybe, they'll treat us to organic 100 per cent durum wheat '0' pasta flour sometime soon.

Another thing I'd like to do is make great organic buckwheat or rice pasta dough. Fresh & Wild do sell buckwheat flour and brown rice flour and I love using them in various different ways – some of which have made it into this little book – but I'd love to find organic buckwheat or brown rice flours specifically milled for home pasta making. That way I'll be able to include buckwheat soba noodle recipes in the next book, or a recipe for glass vermicelli with a great wholegrain texture. Here's wishing ...

CHOCOLATE TAGLIATELLE

with Strawberry Sauce

FOR 4 GENEROUS DESSERT-SIZED SERVINGS:

CHOCOLATE TAGLIATELLE:
250g Dove's Farm 'o' pasta flour
50g cocoa powder
2–3 tablespoons rapadura
3 eggs
2 teaspoons hazelnut oil

Mix the flour, cocoa and rapadura in a bowl, then pour it onto your work surface and make a dip in the middle of the pile. Crack the eggs into the bowl, add the oil and lightly whisk with a fork. Pour this mixture into the dip and, using your fingers, work the flour into the eggs until you have a dough. Alternatively, plonk all the ingredients in a food processor and whizz until it forms a breadcrumb consistency. Bring these crumbs together on a work surface with your hands to form a ball.

So, whether you've used your fingers or a machine, you should now have a ball of dough ready. Now's the time to build up muscle. Knead the dough for a good 5 minutes. If it seems too sticky, add a bit more flour and knead some more. Give it one last knead, then wrap the ball of dough in a clean plastic carrier bag and pop it in the fridge for half an hour.

Put the pasta rollers onto the widest setting and flour well. Cut the dough into four equal pieces. Feed the first piece of dough through, folding it in half. Dust the rollers with flour whenever they lose their coating, and keep folding and rolling the dough a few more times. Keep the work surface floured too.

Move up a notch on the rolling machine, and roll the dough and fold it a few times. Keep raising the notches and rolling in the same way until it's reached about the middle notch, depending on the thickness you want. As the pasta gets thinner, you won't have to do the folding bit, because it will naturally start getting more and more stretchy. I generally go one notch further than the middle, as there's no need to go all the way to the wafer-thin last notch.

Feed the finished sheets of pasta through the machine's cutters to make tagliatelle ribbons, or try cutting them into wavy shapes if you're feeling arty – it's up to you. Whatever style of pasta you cut the sheets into, hang it over the back of a clean chair that has a clean tea towel draped over it, then start again on the next piece of dough. Roll and repeat for the remaining pieces of dough.

The fresh pasta only takes 2–3 minutes to boil, depending on how al dente you like it, so it needs to be put on to boil a couple of minutes before the strawberry tarragon sauce is ready. However, don't leave it hanging around too long if you want to boil it up fresh. After an hour or so, it will be on the way to drying out and becoming the hard stuff you get in packets (if packets of chocolate tagliatelle existed that is).

FOR THE STRAWBERRY SAUCE:

250g fresh strawberries

1 tablespoon rapadura

¼ teaspoon balsamic vinegar

1 whole vanilla pod

A small pinch of black pepper

100ml single cream or soy dream (optional)

This is a good way to use up strawberries that are on the cusp of going too soft. Take the little leaves and stalks off the strawberries, quarter the fruit and put them into a small saucepan with the rapadura, vinegar, vanilla and pepper. Warm on the lowest heat possible, with the lid on, until the strawberries have broken down and combined with the other ingredients, coaxing them every now and then with a wooden spoon.

Now remove the vanilla pod, rinse it under cold water briefly and leave it to dry on your windowsill, ready for another time. Put the cream or soy dream on the table and serve the chocolate pasta on individual plates with strawberry sauce on top.

PS If you want to dry some chocolate pasta for use another day, a strange but genuinely top tip is to buy a broomstick and suspend it horizontally from your kitchen ceiling using cup hooks and string. That way, you can suspend the pasta over the stick so it can dry undisturbed and swinging freely. Alternatively, try an old-fashioned clothes airer, which is just as good, but has the added advantage of looking vintage and fabulous.

BIG ORANGE RAVIOLI

drenched in Hot Chocolate Sauce

Now that we've done chocolate pasta, are you ready for homemade orange lasagne sheets made into ravioli stuffed with orange-flavoured sheep's ricotta cheese, all smothered in a richly hot chocolate sauce?

I'm certain you know all about Green & Black's chocolates, from its creamy white bars to its darkest cooking chocolate, but did you know that it was the first Fairtrade company in the world? Or that it simultaneously made the very first certified organic chocolate in the world? That's a pretty mighty couple of feats there – proper relationships with their growers and lovely relations with us the punters, thanks very much.

You'll have noticed by now that I've written these sweet pasta recipes using a sweetener called rapadura. Rapadura is the same thing as jaggery (rapadura is the South American name and jaggery is the Indian name). Either way, it's simply fresh sugar cane juice that's dried to a rough brown powder. It contains all of the valuable nutrition of sugar cane juice, unlike refined sugar, and also has a flavour a bit like toffee.

Well here goes, tiger ...

BIG ORANGE RAVIOLI

drenched in Hot Chocolate Sauce

DESSERT FOR 6:

RAVIOLI:

200g Dove's Farm 'o' pasta flour

1 tablespoon rapadura

2 eggs

1¼ teaspoons hazelnut oil

Zest of 1 big orange

FILLING:

260g sheep's ricotta cheese

150g mascarpone

40g ground almonds

3 tablespoons freshly squeezed orange juice

2 tablespoons date syrup

Vanilla seeds from one pod

FOR THE SAUCE:

250g Green & Black's cooking chocolate

284ml pot of double cream

Mix the filling ingredients together in a food processor, or in a bowl using a fork.

Make sheets of lasagne by mixing all the pasta ingredients and processing along the same lines as the chocolate tagliatelle recipe (see page 149), but stop when they're still sheets.

Lay the sheets of orange lasagne out on a floured work surface. They'll be about 13cm wide if rolled in a standard machine. Spoon the filling onto the lasagne, a teaspoon at a time, leaving a double sized gap between each spoonful. Moisten the top side of the pasta with a little warm water, then fold the sheet over so that the ricotta is enclosed. Press the top layer down, trying not to get too much air in the little ravioli pockets. With a sharp knife, cut the pasta halfway in between each mound of filling to make big, individual ravioli. Pinch the sides well to keep them watertight.

Break up the chocolate in a plastic bag using a rolling pin or a handy bottle of wine. Put the pieces into a heatproof bowl. Suspend the bowl over a saucepan of boiling water, over a medium heat, and allow the chocolate to melt in the steam. This will take a minute or two.

When the chocolate has totally melted, stir in the cream little by little to make the sauce. In another pan, bring some more water to the boil, then add the ravioli and boil for 4 minutes.

Serve the ravioli piping hot, drenched in the hot chocolate.

AMAZAKE AND APPLE CINNAMON LASAGNE

You might think that sweet pasta is exotic, but you just can't imagine how exotic spaghetti bolognaise was to Londoners in the 1960s – so continental, so chic and so groovy. Italian restaurants in London's Soho provided the first inkling of modern dining patterns.

Before the spaghetti houses arrived, the choice was between take-away fish and chips or an extremely fancy and expensive place called a restaurant, where you got to go on your birthday. Immigrant families from Italy turned that around for us, providing inexpensive and great quality meals that people could eat almost any day. Had a long day? Go get some pasta.

These culinary pioneers also paved the way for all the other fab cuisines that are now enjoyed here in Old Blighty. From Bangladeshi curries to Vietnamese stir-fries, it all began with pasta. So, in just a couple of generations, we've gone from meat and two veg to Amazake and Apple Cinnamon Lasagne. Amazing, innit?

Okay, this is the last of my dessert pasta recipes for this book, and it's a bit of a favourite. You really can't go wrong with the natural sweetness of amazake and cinnamon complementing the familiar bite of Bramley apples. It's lovely served cold the next day too, especially for breakfast.

AMAZAKE AND APPLE CINNAMON LASAGNE

DESSERT FOR 6–8 PEOPLE:

LASAGNE:

150g Dove's Farm 'o' pasta flour

50g chestnut flour

2 eggs

2 tablespoons rapadura

½ teaspoon hazelnut oil

2 teaspoons ground cinnamon

FOR THE SAUCES:

3–4 medium Bramley apples, cored and sliced

A handful of big juicy sultanas

2–3 tablespoons maple syrup, to taste

380g jar of amazake, either traditional rice amazake or millet amazake

Make the lasagne along the same lines as the chocolate tagliatelle recipe (see page 149), but instead of putting it through the tagliatelle cutter attachment, cut the sheets into 30cm lengths of lasagne.

Heat the oven to 180°C/350°F/Gas Mark 4.

Over a very low heat, gently cook the apple slices with a tablespoon of cold water in a covered saucepan. They will take about 10 minutes to go mushy. When they have, stir in the sultanas, 150ml of water and the maple syrup. Test a little bit for sweetness, adding a bit more maple syrup if you think it needs it.

Pour half the apple sauce into a shallow 20cm x 30cm lasagne dish, spread it into an even layer and cover with two sheets of cinnamon pasta, overlapping them side by side to form a layer. Pour on top half the amazake, spread out evenly, then cover with another layer of pasta. Repeat this process, then top the dish with a final layer of pasta for a crispy lid. Bake in the oven for about 20–25 minutes, until golden brown, and serve with Greek yogurt.

GREEN APPLE, GREEN GRAPE

and Gin Jelly

Agar-agar – so good they named it twice. Forget nasty old gelatine, which is made from boiled pigs trotters, agar-agar is used to set this jelly. These creamy white flakes are starchy and snow-like, and can be used instead of gelatine in anything from jellies to quiches. It starts off as a Japanese sea vegetable, which is like dulse or Irish moss. It's boiled and then frozen into a block, which is then shaved to make the flakes. And not only is it vegetarian, but it's actually supremely good for you and naturally high in fibre.

I'm not sure if the same could strictly be claimed for the gin in this jelly, but hey-ho, let's stick it in anyways – especially as it's one of the most awesome gins you have ever tried. You might not even like gin, but you'll like this stuff. Juniper Green Organic Gin is the only gin that can really call itself London gin, as it's the only one, organic or not, that's distilled and bottled in London – in Clapham, actually.

It's the product of the eighth gin-maker in a direct line from the founder of the Thames distillery that produces it. So the current owner of Thames distillery, Charles Maxwell, is the great-great-great-great-great-grandson of the original founder, George Bishop. And it seems that Charles's great-great-great-great-great-grandfather handed down some seriously secret recipes for the most gorgeous gins, with each generation passing it on to the next.

With any kind of craft, **experience is the key** – and learning hands on from someone who knows.

So it's little wonder that Juniper Green is a smooth, fragrant and very special spirit that'll warm your cockles. And, of course, flavour your jelly with its unique blend of juniper, coriander, angelica and savory.

The orange zest in this recipe adds a tiny bit of flavour, but is mostly there to add pretty, speckledy bits that form a little orange cosmos of zesty stars on top of the finished jelly. The grated green apple floats to the top of the liquid jelly, so when it's turned out, the apple forms the jelly base. All in all, the layered fruit look lovely, the apple juice provides lots of sweetness and the gin makes this dessert fragrant, delicious and nicely alcoholic.

It's grown-up jelly. **Enjoy.**

GREEN APPLE, GREEN GRAPE
and Gin Jelly

MAKES 4 INDIVIDUAL JELLIES OR 1 BIG JELLY:

16 green grapes, halved and de-seeded
400ml pressed apple juice
250ml water
Zest of ¼ an orange, finely grated
5 tablespoons agar-agar flakes, plus an extra teaspoon if you like firm jelly
1 green eating apple
6 tablespoons gin

Put the grapes into jelly moulds. You can get lovely ones from antique shops and flea markets. I've used little 1930's moulds, bought from Bermondsey Antiques Market, for this recipe when making individual-sized jellies, or a big glass Victorian jelly mould I found in Hastings for the one full-sized, made-to-share jelly. Alternatively, you can simply use some little bowls or ramekins. What's needed is a mould or moulds of some sort that will contain about 800ml when filled to the top or divided between them all. Of course, individual smaller moulds will set the jelly more quickly than one big one.

Pour the juice, water and the zest of the orange into a small saucepan. Scatter the agar-agar into the pan, but don't stir. Place on a medium heat until it simmers. Simmer for about 3 minutes, stirring now and then.

Grate the apple and put it into the mould or moulds, on top of the grapes. Take the agar-agar off the heat once it's done and stir in the gin. Pour equal amounts of the hot jelly into each bowl and leave to cool down for about an hour. Stick the jelly into the fridge once it's cold and leave it to set for a good couple of hours. Serve with frozen yogurt, hemp ice cream or clotted cream.

RICE PUDDING

with Rosy Dates

Deeply old-fashioned, the original rice pudding concept was brought from India and the Middle East to Europe by colonial Victorian Brits, along with tea and sugar. My rice pudding recipe's got a twist, as it's made with an ancient form of Japanese rice called sweet rice, although it's not very sweet. It is high in protein, so it has a particularly sticky texture when cooked. Rose water, almonds, dates and spices are also included, giving a Middle Eastern flavour.

I've used rice milk for this rice pudding recipe because cream is one of the other ingredients. To have both cow's milk and cream would amount to a lot of cow. Although I eat virtually everything these days (so long as it's organic or decent), I think there's a lot to be said for moderation. After all, drinking cow's milk is a strange thing for adult human beings to do. No other mammal keeps on suckling after it's grown up and no other mammal steals milk from another species. And in fact, most human cultures don't do it either, in particular the vast majority of the Far East and many tropical cultures.

I treat milky things as a big fat treat. They're not everyday, all-the-time foods, but a now and then, a couple of times a week, oh-go-on-in-tea sort of thing. And seeing as there's already cream in this recipe and milk made out of rice tastes great, it's my hands-down favourite choice for this rice pudding.

Flower waters are a wonderful way of adding summer fragrances to winter meals. Fresh & Wild sell rose water in some of their stores, but you might want to try your hand at making your own. Simply get a cup full of rose petals from an organic souce, like your garden, and simmer them in a cup and a half of water for about 10 minutes. Strain to remove the petals, and keep the rose water in the fridge for up to a week. You can also store some frozen in ice cube trays. Come mid-winter, add ice cubes of rose water to different dishes, from desserts like this to savoury rices. They'll melt and release the fragrance of warm sunny days.

On a cold winter's night, **rice pudding delivers delicious comfort**. In summer, it's good served cold with a fruit salad.

At any time of the year, it's an excellent pre-gig treat, especially when flavoured with a swirl of organic fruit purée or fruit spread – great stodge to keep you on your toes all night.

Vanilla is an important ingredient in this recipe. After years at the back of the cupboard, it became fashionable again just as Madagascar had a succession of terrible hurricane disasters a couple of years ago. As the Western world remembered the joys of real dried vanilla pods, many of the farms where they were grown were decimated. And as a cyclical crop, the disturbance to the cycle might take some time to sort out.

Thankfully, we'll not easily forget these softly flavoured elegant pods again, so the Madagascan farmers are able to rebuild their livelihoods with lots of demand to support them. Meanwhile, there are also some new tropical suppliers who are beginning to send their wares our way.

Check out Fairtrade Indonesian, Mexican and Reunion vanilla pods when they appear. They've got quite different flavour profiles and cooking characteristics, in the same way that different varieties of chilli have wildy varying tastes.

Fruit spreads are, to my mind, proper jams, but they're not allowed to be called that by law. If jam-makers put too much lovely fresh fruit and not enough sugar into their jams, they've legally got to call them fruit spreads. So opt for fruit spreads if you want jams with extra fruit, but remember to store them in the fridge, as the lack of sugar to preserve them means they'll spoil in the cupboard just like squashed fruit would.

On the pomegranate front, choose firm fruit during their brief autumn season, but pick out the beautiful jewel-coloured seeds with care. The pretty yellow membrane stuff tastes foul, so don't spoil your pudding with any stray scraps.

This rice pudding recipe is properly 'ricey'. I've tried a lot of rice puddings that are thin and milky with a few bits of rice bobbing about in them, but this one's quite thick and substantial. You might prefer adding some more rice milk, after the cream's gone in, for a thinner pudding, but I'll have mine unadulterated please. It'd go very gloopy if you left it to go cold, but there's fat chance of that, 'cause it's creamy, rosy, gorgeous.

RICE PUDDING WITH ROSY DATES

TO SERVE 4–5 PEOPLE:

8 pitted dates, chopped
125ml rose water
100g whole grain Japanese sweet rice
750ml rice drink
2 x 284ml pots of single cream
1 dried vanilla pod
4 cardamom pods
4 tablespoons ground almonds
4 tablespoons flaked almonds
Fruit purée or fruit spread to taste
A few pomegranate seeds

Put the dates into a bowl and pour in the rose water. Leave to soak for as long as possible, preferably overnight, but an hour will do. Wash the rice in cold water. Pour the rice and the rice milk into a medium saucepan and slowly bring to the boil over a medium heat. Lower the heat until the rice is gently simmering, then cook with the lid on for about 40 minutes, stirring once halfway through so that it doesn't stick to the bottom of the pan.

Add the cream, vanilla pod, cardamom pods, ground and flaked almonds and the dates, and continue to simmer, without the lid on, stirring now and then to stop the pudding sticking. After about 10–15 minutes, take the pudding off the heat. Fish out the vanilla pod, rinse it and leave it out to dry for another time. Serve the rice pudding in bowls swirled with spirals of fruit purée or fruit spread and sprinkled with pomegranate seeds.

JANET'S ICE CREAM

Janet and Ross Anderson live at East Lochhead, a Scottish farm by a loch, near Glasgow. I first visited them care of sustainable tourism specialists Natural Discovery, and think of the farm as a little bolt hole away from hectic city life. Janet and Ross keep traditional Highland cattle, with ginger woolly mammoth-style coats and big macho horns, plus heirloom black and white Jacob's sheep, some old ponies, a pack of dogs, a sweet cat and loads of chickens and ducks.

They really are living their own version of the Good Life, constantly tending to the flocks, growing berries and turnips, or knitting and wearing jumpers and scarves out of their own home-dyed wool. They run the farm as a guesthouse too, winning awards for sustainability and top marks for the home-grown food that they serve. Here's Janet's recipe for ice cream, which not only tastes outrageously good, but doesn't need an ice cream maker. You simply stick it in the freezer, then serve it after dinner or at teatime on a hot summer's day.

JANET'S **ICE CREAM**

TO MAKE A BIG TUB OF RICH ICE CREAM YOU WILL NEED:

2 egg whites

175g rapadura

6 tablespoons water

300ml whipping cream

FLAVOURING OF YOUR CHOICE, E.G.:

Broken white chocolate

Fruit compote

Brandy

Cherry Chocolate Spread (see page 275) before it's put in the fridge

Strawberry Sauce (see page 151) when it's cooled down

Beat the egg whites using an electric whisk. Continue whizzing until they're stiff and form peaks.

Make a syrup by putting the rapadura and water into a heavy-based pan and heating slowly, over a low heat, to dissolve the grains. Stir occasionally with a wooden spoon. As the rapadura dissolves, brush down the sides of the pan with a pastry brush dipped in cold water to remove any stray grains. Don't allow the syrup to boil until every grain of sugar has dissolved. Once all the rapadura has dissolved, increase the heat and bring the syrup to a foaming boil. Boil vigorously for 2 minutes.

Pour the boiling sugar syrup onto the egg whites in a steady thin stream, beating until the mixture is smooth and glossy. Whip the cream, then fold it into the mixture. Pour into a 2-litre plastic tub and freeze.

About 6–7 hours later, get the tub out of the freezer. The mixture should be pretty frozen on the outside, but not solid in the middle yet. Scrape all of the mixture into a big mixing bowl using a fork, then whisk it well using an electric whisk if you have one, or a fork if you don't. The idea is to break down all of the ice crystals to make a smooth and creamy ice cream.

If you're going to, now's the time to add any flavourings. Mix them in quickly, then pour the mixture back into the plastic tub. The content will have gone down to almost half the amount. Freeze it again and eat anytime after another 10–12 hours, and up to a couple of months. You'll probably only need small servings – it's so rich and creamy a little goes a long way.

POACHED **QUINCES**

In medieval times, quinces were eaten by lovers, served at weddings and given as romantic gifts. Originating in Persia, and popular in Greece and southern Europe, quinces are undergoing a bit of a comeback here in the UK. They're in season throughout the autumn, which is perfect, as they're always eaten cooked or made into preserves.

Quinces are hard, yellow fruit that look a bit like mouldy apples. They aren't the prettiest of fruit, being naturally lumpier and bumpier than most modern beauties, but when cooked they have a firm but succulent texture, a highly perfumed and exotic flavour and go a gorgeous spectrum of colours, from orange to pink. Don't worry about the blemishes on the skin – that's normal and the blemishes don't affect their deliciousness.

Store quinces in a plastic bag in the fridge, where they'll last for up to two months. They make lovely gifts for loved ones when poached and bottled. Simply boil an old jam jar in water to sterilize it, then spoon in the cooked quinces. Put the lid on and decorate with a ribbon.

When quinces aren't in season, use this recipe, minus the syrup, to poach apples and pears – you only need about 5 minutes for apples and a couple for pears. Any longer than that and they'll disintegrate into a compote, which is also lovely, but different to poached fruit.

P O A C H E D **QUINCES**

FOR 6 SMALL PORTIONS:

500g quinces, peeled, cored and cut into crescent moons
300ml date syrup
100ml red wine
7g cassia bark
1 star anise
1 bay leaf

Put everything into a pan and stir with a wooden spoon, over a low heat, for 4–5 minutes. Put the lid on the pan and simmer it for about half an hour. Using a knife, see if the quinces are really soft, pink and ready. Cook them some more if they need it, still with the lid on. They can be served warm, but I generally prefer them cold with hot custard or Janet's Ice Cream (see page 167).

ROOIBOSCH TEA CAKES

These cakes are made by soaking dried fruit in rooibosch tea. Naturally caffeine free, rooibosch is high in antioxidants and flavour. It's a good starter tea if you're new to herb teas, as it's best drunk with milk, soy milk or lemon, just like standard teas. You can adapt this recipe by soaking the fruit in fruit teas to add different flavours.

Instead of using dried fruit like raisins and sultanas, try Tropical Wholefoods fairly-traded tropical fruits, Crazy Jack's soft-dried fruits, or slow-dried fruit from Southern Alps – if you can manage to get them into the cake mix before they disappear. I strongly believe that if it's mid-winter and you're missing summer fruits like strawberries, the only way forward is to eat preserved summer fruits. That means strawberry jams, frozen compotes and purées, or slow-dried strawberries.

There's tons more flavour in these options than the airsick strawberries that have been picked too young and flown, in the freezing cold, halfway round the world. Poor things, stop picking on them and eat preserved ones from summer instead. And have you ever wondered if people are taking advantage out of the workers in Kenya who grow summer fruits for us during our winter? I just get the feeling they're getting paid a lot less than European farmers do to grow the same crops in our summertime.

There's simply no need for it, especially with the quality of the dried fruits that are now finding their way to these shores. Take Crazy Jack's soft-dried

Calimyrna figs from Anatolia in Turkey. In fact, forget these little juicy numbers even have the words 'fig' or 'dried' in their name. Focus on the word 'soft' and you'll begin to get the right idea about their succulence, sweetness and sexiness. They bear no relation whatsoever to the crusty, dusty dried figs of yesteryear and instead are fragrant and juicy – which is why I've only listed 100g of figs in this recipe, leaving a generous 150g out of the 250g packet for you to enjoy as soon as it's opened.

Likewise, Tropical Wholefood's chewy banana chips have a lovely texture that is, just like it says, chewy – and banana-y. That's more than you can say for old-fashioned dried banana chips. And let's not forget the sun-dried papaya and star fruit – both are great and are way better than any standard dried versions of these you may have tried. The same goes for the dried pineapple in Southern Alp's dried fruit mix. The pineapple rings are much more tart than you'd expect – none of this strange sugary candied stuff that we used to be forced to deal with back in the old days. Instead their dried pineapple tastes entirely of the very best tropical pineapples. Amazing!

With all this flavour hanging around in my Rooibosch Tea Cakes, what's needed is a quality spice mix that can handle the competition and rise to complement such strong, sophisticated succulence. Seasoned Pioneers' little parcels of exotica are incredibly varied, and can handle sweet jobs just as ably as savoury moments. The Ras-el-Hanout mix contains everything from rosebuds to galangal, expertly blended to give your cooking a true taste of Morocco. So forget that it's a savoury rice spice and whack it into this cake.

Serve Rooibosch Tea Cakes with lemon crème fraîche, or Seville orange crème fraîche during its short January season.

ROOIBOSCH TEA CAKES

TO MAKE ABOUT 20 LITTLE BROWNIE-SIZED CAKE BLOCKS:

100g Crazy Jack's soft-dried figs

50g Tropical Wholefoods chewy banana chips

50g Tropical Wholefoods sun-dried papaya

50g Tropical Wholefoods sun-dried star fruit

65g Southern Alps slow-dried fruit mix

300ml rooibosch or fruit tea of your choice

250g wholemeal flour

2 teaspoon Seasoned Pioneers Ras-el-Hanout spice blend

2 teaspoons baking powder

50g rapadura

4 eggs, beaten

150g raisins

FOR THE CRÈME FRAÎCHE:

250ml pot of crème fraîche

Zest of one washed lemon or the zest of ¼ a washed Seville orange

Soak the figs, bananas, papaya and star fruit, plus the mango, apple, jumbo raisins and the pineapple from the Southern Alps mix, overnight in the rooibosch or fruit tea of your choice.

Next day, grease a 30cm × 20cm roasting tin, and set the oven to 160°C/325°F/Gas Mark 3. Chop the soaked fruit. Mix the flour, spices, baking powder and rapadura together in a bowl, then add the egg, the soaked fruit, the raisins and any tea that's not soaked into the fruit, and mix well. Pour the mixture into the tin. If it's too thick for this, mix in a bit of milk or rice milk, then pour it into the tin.

Bake in the middle of the oven for about 45 minutes, or until a knife, inserted into the middle of the cake, comes out clean. During this time, you can eat the slow-dried strawberries out of the fruit mix to congratulate yourself for not picking at the dried fruit in the cake.

When the cake is ready, take it out of the oven, but leave it in the tin for a few minutes. Then turn it out onto a cold grill tray to cool. Once it's cold, slice the big cake into five along its length and four along its width, making 20 little brownie-style cake blocks. Mix the fruit zest and crème fraîche and serve the cake with a generous dollop.

ORANGE, ALMOND AND BRANDY TARTS

These little babies are quick to make and are guaranteed to impress your friends. Try adding lemon rind and juice instead of orange for lemon tarts, squashing in ripe strawberries for strawberry tarts, mincing in some fresh pineapple for pineapple tarts, dropping in some almond essence for almond tarts ... it all depends on the season and your *preferences du jour.*

FOR 12 MINI TARTS:

100g plain white flour

75g plain wholemeal flour

50g rapadura

75g butter or vegan margarine that's suitable for baking

2 tablespoon orange juice squeezed out of the big orange

FOR THE FILLING:

Grated zest of 1 big orange and juice of half of it

250g plain tofu

40g ground almonds

2 tablespoons agave syrup

1 tablespoon brandy

First make the pastry by mixing the flours and rapadura in a bowl, then rubbing the fat in with your fingers. The secret of good pastry is to use butter or marg that's at room temperature, and fingers that are a bit cold. Use an upward motion with your fingers but don't let the mixture touch your hot palms as it crumbles. When it has turned to crumbs, mix in the 2 tablespoons of orange juice, knead it into a dough and then squash it together into a ball. Grease a 12-hole bun tray. Divvy the dough into twelve pieces, roll each bit into a ball and squash each one into a flat circle. Press each piece into each dip in the bun tray and up the sides, so you end up with 12 empty tart cases. Pop the tray into the fridge for 20 minutes while you go and read the paper/play with your kids/have a bath, then put the oven on to 190°C/375°F/Gas Mark 5. Bake the tarts for about 15 minutes, so that they're just golden brown.

Turn off the oven and get the tart cases out. Let them cool in their tray for 5 minutes, then gently turn them out to fully cool.

Now it's filling time. Place the grated orange zest and the juice of half the orange in a food processor. Wash the tofu under the cold tap, then put it into the food processor along with the remaining filling ingredients. Zap, then zap some more until everything is creamy.

Spoon the filling into the tarts, pat it down and chill the tarts in the fridge for at least an hour. Serve with mint tea and fresh fruit.

AMAZAKE CHOCOLATE CAKE

The slightly scary surprise ingredient in this fabulous cake is courgette. Although everybody's eaten carrot cake these days, most people seem pretty dubious if you suggest that any other vegetables might be nice in cakes. The courgettes are added purely to enhance the texture of this moist confectionery.

As for the amazake, I bet you the rest of the jar doesn't quite make it back into the fridge. It's true that amazake is supremely good for you, with its slow-releasing sugars, but amazake is so completely delicious that it would remain popular in my kitchen even if it wasn't so healthy. Advieh is a delicate Iranian spice blend made from cinnamon, cardamom, cumin and rose petals. Generally used to flavour savoury rice dishes, it's used here to gently fragrance and intensify the chocolate.

This recipe also contains wheat germ. Whole wheat grains are made up of an outer coating of bran, an inner layer of wheat germ, and the inside kernel of the grain which is called the endosperm. Whilst bran is the bit which is highest in fibre and contains most of the minerals and vitamins, wheat germ is packed with the stress-busting B vitamins, cancer-protecting vitamin E and selenium, blood-boosting iron, and buckets of protein. And whilst eating too much bran on its own can actually inhibit your absorption of some nutrients, eating more wheat germ is a great thing to do. So now you can have your cake and eat it.

AMAZAKE CHOCOLATE CAKE

FOR 1 TEA PARTY-SIZED CAKE:

1 vanilla pod

1 egg

170g amazake – either rice amazake or millet amazake

3 tablespoons sunflower oil

3 tablespoons hempseed oil

2 tablespoons agave syrup

115g spelt flour

15g cocoa powder

40g wheat germ

1¼ teaspoons baking powder

¼ teaspoon advieh spice blend or cinnamon

1 medium courgette

60g decent milk chocolate, chopped

Grease a 19cm loose-bottomed, deep cake tin. Turn the oven on to 180°C/350°F/Gas Mark 4. Split the vanilla pod with a very sharp knife, then scrape the seeds into a mixing bowl. Beat the vanilla seeds with the egg, amazake, both the oils and the agave syrup, using a hand whisk.

In another bowl, mix the flour, cocoa, wheat germ, baking powder and spices. Top and tail, then grate the courgette. Stir the flour mixture into the amazake mixture, then fold in the courgette and chocolate pieces. Pour into the tin and bake for about an hour. Insert a metal skewer into the centre of the cake to check if it's cooked. It will come out clean if the cake is ready. Leave the cake to cool in the tin for 15 minutes, then turn out onto a wire grill rack to cool completely.

SOUPS & SALADS

John Hurd
Organic Watercress Company, Hill Deverill, Wiltshire

'Watercress contains more Vitamin C than fresh oranges, and more calcium than cow's milk – in fact it's one of the best ACE foods around. It's such a tasty little plant, one that has hardly changed since the days of the Ancient Romans.'

S O U P S

The original liquid lunch, or dinner for that matter, soups are comfort food and quick and easy, too.

Here are eight soups with eight very different approaches. There's a fish chowder, a thick pulsey soup, a rich meaty soup, a miso soup, a creamy squash soup, a milky consommé, a noodle soup and a mushroom broth.

These are eight corkers, exploring eight very different soup moments, from starter to main meal.

F & W SMOKED SALMON CHOWDER

Salmon are very sensitive creatures, with unusual habits and behaviour patterns. For starters, although they're born and bred in freshwater rivers, young salmon migrate to the sea to live in salt water for most of their lives. There have been lots of scares about intensively farmed, non-organic salmon being bad for our health. If you know a little about how they're farmed, you'll understand why non-organic salmon just isn't a good idea. Basically, it can be a bit like battery-farm eggs, but at times even worse.

When you keep animals and fish in overcrowded and unsanitary conditions, they're prone to getting sick through stress and disease. Human beings would suffer the same fate if they were forced to live fifty to a house for the whole of their lives. They'd pass loads of bugs between themselves, get very stressed and miserable, get into fights and generally be in poor shape from lack of exercise. So is it any wonder that non-organic salmon, which are forced to live in the equivalent of a bathtub of water in a sea cage with up to fifty thousand other fish, don't provide the best food? They have to be regularly de-liced with pesticides that are known chemical nerve toxins, are fed weird industrial fishmeal full of chemicals and colourants, and often attack each other because they're so distressed.

Organic salmon farms are much better places, because organic farming guidelines were built with animal welfare in mind, as well as human and environmental needs. The fish have more space to move and exhibit their natural behaviour, making them less stressed, happier and healthier. And that has to be nicer for them and better for us. They're fed trimmings from fish for human consumption, such as the bits cut off of plaice when it's filleted. They're only ever given veterinary drugs if they get sick, not as a regular preventative dosing, and, if they do get sick, the certification inspectors have to attend to check the treatment process.

It's little wonder then that organic smoked salmon has a much more delicate taste and appearance than intensively farmed, non-organic salmon. It is 'salmon' pink instead of the garishly bright tan colour of non-organic smoked salmon. And it's usually gently smoked over oak charcoals for a rounder, smoky flavour.

Fish chowders are a good way to make the most of this expensive ingredient, as a little goes a long way to produce a **full-flavoured soup**.

I've adapted Diana Cooper's original Fresh & Wild recipe to suit a home kitchen, but it's essentially the same as the Fresh & Wild classic. Try floating a blob of goat's yogurt or crème fraîche on top and sprinkling over some fresh chopped chives.

F & W SMOKED SALMON CHOWDER

TO SERVE 4 AS A STARTER:

A knob of butter
2 small onions, peeled and finely chopped
2 medium floury potatoes, scrubbed and diced into 2cm-ish cubes
600ml full cream milk
Black pepper to taste
600g Joubere (or 600ml homemade) vegetable stock
100g smoked salmon or gravadlax, finely chopped
2 handfuls of fresh dill or tarragon, finely chopped

Melt the butter in a saucepan, over a medium heat, then add the onion and fry until softened, being careful not to let it go brown. Add the potato, milk, a pinch of pepper and the stock after a few minutes. Lower the heat and simmer for about 10 minutes. Add the salmon and fresh herbs and keep simmering for a further 5 minutes. Taste and add a little more pepper if necessary.

F&W MINTED GREEN PEA SOUP

This soup is a classic from the team at Fresh & Wild's central kitchen. The dried peas are hearty, protein-rich warmers that are lightened up by the mint. The cumin adds a little hint of exoticism to this filling soup.

TO SERVE 2 AS A DINNER:

1 medium onion, peeled and chopped
1 tablespoon sunflower oil
½ teaspoon ground cumin
150g split green peas
750g Joubere (or 750ml homemade) vegetable stock
A handful of fresh mint, finely chopped
Sea salt and pepper to taste

In a medium saucepan, fry the onion in the oil, over a medium heat, until it's translucent. Add the cumin, fry for 20–30 seconds and then add the dried peas and stock. Put a lid on the pan and simmer the soup for about half an hour. Give it a stir to see if all the peas are nice and mushy. If it's ready, throw in the mint. After about a minute, take the soup off the heat and add salt and pepper to taste. Serve with Phat Green Flat Bread (see recipe page 242), or hot buttered rolls.

PROPER BEEFY ONION SOUP

with Alpine le Gruyère Cheese

This soup is a classic example of why organic is best. From the sweetness of the onions, to the full flavour of the organic beef stock and the tastiness of the traditionally-crafted cheese, this is fine artisan dining.

For flavour, healthiness and animal welfare reasons, proper French-with-a-twist **onion soup simply** has to be **artisan and organic**.

French people much prefer Swiss le gruyère over their homegrown French gruyère – and that's not a typo. The French version is just gruyère, whereas the Swiss version has a fanfare – in the form of a 'le' – before its name.

Why? Because mountain cows in the Swiss Alps graze on summer meadows full of wild weeds, and these alpine meadow flowers, grasses and herbs give their milk a delicate and delicious flavour. And it's this milk that gives le gruyère cheese its characteristic perfume and tang.

Hand-crafted le gruyère comes in massive 35-kilo wheels, each one made out of at least 400 litres of alpine milk. Medieval Swiss farmers started making this cheese because their mountain homes were so remote. During the winter, it was impossible for them to travel to the nearest market, so they needed to find a way to collectively pool their resources to make a nutritious food that could keep them over the cold months.

Each spring they would heat all their milk together in a copper cauldron until it curdled, strain the liquid out of the solids using a massive piece of cheesecloth and put the curds into a 60cm wide wooden hoop to set. Two grown men were then needed to lift the young cheese into a specially hewn cave in the mountains, where it was left to mature over the summer, ready for eating in autumn.

This age-old process is still used today for the le gruyère on sale in Fresh & Wild, and also for the French gruyère that comes from the other side of the same Jura mountains.

PROPER BEEFY ONION SOUP

with Alpine le Gruyère Cheese

ENOUGH FOR LUNCH FOR 4:

2 tablespoons butter

14 medium-sized onions, peeled and chopped

2 teaspoons dried rosemary

2 teaspoons dried thyme

2 teaspoons cider vinegar

2 teaspoons rapadura

10g powdered kuzu or plain white flour

125ml white wine

1 litre homemade beef stock or 900g (3 pots) Joubere organic beef stock

Crushed black pepper to taste

TOASTS:

4 slices of yesterday's bread, preferably white

2 garlic cloves, crushed

2 teaspoons French mustard

100g Swiss Alpine le gruyère cheese, grated

Heat the butter in a medium-sized saucepan, over a medium heat, and add the onions when it's melted. Fry and stir with a wooden spoon for about 5 minutes, then throw in the herbs, put the lid on the pan and turn the heat down to the lowest setting. Leave the onions to sauté for half an hour.

Turn the heat up a little, but only a little – it should still be low. Uncover the pan and stir in the vinegar and rapadura. Keep stirring the onions until they've gone an appetizing, caramelized brown. This will take about a quarter of an hour. You can't rush this, as the onion-browning part of this recipe is vital if the bitter onions are to turn mellow and sweet.

When they're finally done, stir in the kuzu or flour. Keep stirring and cooking for a couple of minutes, then add the wine. Give it a good stir to make sure no lumps appear and then add the stock little by little. Sprinkle a pinch of pepper into the soup, put the lid back on and leave to simmer for another quarter of an hour.

Turn the grill on and lightly toast the bread. When it's done, spread the garlic and mustard evenly between the slices, but don't turn the grill off.

When the soup's cooked, ladle it into four heatproof bowls and float a piece of toast on each, garlic side up. Divvy up the cheese, sprinkle it on top of the toast floats and then put the bowls under the grill. Let the cheese properly melt over the soup, then serve.

REAL MISO SOUP

You can find packets of ready-made miso soup at Fresh & Wild – and they're brilliant for elevenses, travelling, post-clubbing, post-gym and a post-anything else quick fix – but to be honest, proper home-made miso soup is damn quick and easy to make from scratch. You can make it *very* simple, or add different vegetables, tofus, seafood, noodles and garnishes to make a meal of things. This recipe's a good starting place – a simple and traditional miso broth with added carrots, chard and spring onions.

To make the broth you need to add dashi to miso. Dashi is an ancient Japanese vegetable stock made from the sea vegetable kombu and hot water, with nothing else added. It's got to be the world's easiest stock to make, right up there with instant cubes and powders in terms of easiness, and with fine restaurant stocks in terms of taste, purity and class. It keeps for about a week in the fridge and freezes well, so I usually make it in big batches and freeze it in 500ml pots for future use.

Miso is a paste made by fermenting soy beans with salt and usually grains. There are loads of different kinds of miso, from sweet white miso to full-bodied dark brown hatcho miso. Generally, they divide up into mellow misos and dark misos, with the darker varieties having more savoury and earthier flavours. It's a bit like red and white wines, with lots of different varieties of miso being classed as mellow or dark. All misos are full of healing isoflavones and all are strongly flavoured foods. Miso should never ever be boiled up in a soup, as this destroys the good bacterial culture and the balance of flavours. Instead, add a little of the cooked liquid to the miso to dissolve it, pour this liquor back into the soup and then serve it without any further cooking.

REAL MISO SOUP

MISO SOUP FOR 4 PEOPLE:

20cm piece of dried kombu

2 big chard leaves, washed

1 carrot, scrubbed, topped, tailed and sliced into julienne strips

2 small spring onions, trimmed and finely chopped

4 tablespoons dark miso of your choice, such as mugi or hatcho

The first part of this recipe is for the main kind of stock used in Japanese cuisine, called dashi. To make it, boil the kombu and 1 litre of water in a large saucepan, over a medium heat, for at least 20 minutes. If you want a stronger dashi, boil it for a bit longer. Take the kombu out of the pan and leave it to dry. (You can add it to beans and pulses when you next cook them, as it'll make them easier to digest.) You now have a classic dashi.

Chop the stems off the chard leaves, then halve the leaves down the central rib. Finely chop the leaves and the stems into separate piles. Throw the carrot into the dashi and simmer for a couple of minutes. Throw the chopped chard stem in next and cook for a minute more. Add the spring onion and the chard leaves and simmer for another minute or two. Turn the heat off.

Put the miso into a ceramic bowl and spoon a couple of tablespoons of the broth in. Dissolve the miso paste by squashing it about the bowl with a teaspoon or chopsticks, adding more broth if you need it. Add this diluted miso liquid to the main soup and stir it in well.

You can serve this at just about any time of day. Drink it with a slurp out of Japanese rice bowls, chopsticks at the ready, or Western-style with spoons.

JAPANESE SQUASH SOUP

Most adults in this country didn't eat pumpkin or squash when they were growing up. And if they did, it was usually a once a year experience – eating the remains of the Hallowe'en lantern, with remnants of greasepaint on your face and the smell of autumn leaves and bonfires on the wind.

It's hardly surprising then that while lots of people like the look of all the exotic and richly-coloured varieties you can now get, they don't always give them a go. Just what are you meant to do with these strange vegetables?

Well actually, you can do just about anything. They're good baked and fried, stewed and curried, roasted and raw, mashed and juiced, steamed and sautéed. There's a salad recipe for them on page 224, a recipe for the seeds on page 315, and they're especially lovely in soups.

I picked up this recipe on a trip to Japan, where squashes are an integral part of the cuisine. It's very creamy and sweet for a savoury soup and can be made with deep orange-red kuri, gourd-shaped butternut, or kabocha squashes, with their jade green stripy skins and peachy-coloured flesh. The texture is the thing that varies most, with red kuri breaking down into a velvet-like consistency, and butternut and kabocha remaining slightly firmer.

When choosing the squash, get one that feels heavy for its size. Also, the best butternut squashes are the ones with a more slender round end.

The **less roundness**, the **less seeds** and the more flesh. Experiment and get the squash that **looks best** on the day.

If you fancy adding some dairy, use butter instead of the sunflower oil and dairy cream instead of soya cream. And if you're serving this soup as a main meal, try throwing in 400g of fresh or defrosted shrimps or prawns – simply add them to the pan along with the shallots.

JAPANESE SQUASH SOUP

TO SERVE 4–6 PEOPLE:

1 red kuri, butternut or kabocha squash
4–6 shallots, depending on the size of the squash
4–6cm piece fresh ginger root, depending on the size of the pumpkin
2 tablespoons sunflower oil
1 tablespoon toasted sesame oil
¼ nutmeg, finely grated
400ml coconut milk
1 litre carton unsweetened soy milk
4–6 tablespoons white miso, depending on the size of the pumpkin
6 tablespoons soya cream
A handful of fresh chives, finely chopped

Cut the woody stalk off the squash and slice from top to bottom. With your fingers and a tablespoon, scrape out the seeds and put them in a bowl for another time. (There's a recipe for them on page 315.) Most squashes can be used without peeling, but the skins get thicker as the season goes on. If your squash seems to have a hard skin, then peel it. When in doubt, leave it on and cook a little longer.

Chop the squash into 3cm-ish cubes using a big sharp knife. When it's all prepped, imagine the chunks in soup bowls and work out how many bowls of soup it would make. Peel, halve and chop the same number of shallots and grate the same number of centimetres of ginger. Heat the oils in a large saucepan, over a medium heat, and add the shallots, ginger and nutmeg when it's hot. Fry for a couple of minutes, stirring with a wooden spoon, then add the squash.

Keep frying for a minute, still stirring, and then pour in the coconut milk. Add enough soy milk to cover the squash and bring to a simmer. Put the lid on the pan and turn the heat down so that it doesn't boil over but keeps simmering. Check how soft the squash is after about 20 minutes. If it's very soft and creamy, take the soup off the heat. If it's not quite there, put the lid back on and leave it for another 10 minutes or so.

When the squash is cooked, turn the heat off. Put the miso in a bowl, measuring out the same number of tablespoons as the number of servings of soup you're making. With a tablespoon, take some of the hot coconut broth and add it to the miso. Mix it in, then repeat five or six times until the miso has turned from a paste into a thick liquid.

Pour this liquid into the saucepan and stir it in. Now pour as much of the soup as will fit, into a liquidizer and zap it. Do this again to liquidize the remaining soup, transferring each batch into another container to make space for the next lot. If you don't have a liquidizer or food processor, simply pour the soup into a sieve over another big saucepan or bowl and, using a spoon, squash the pumpkin through the sieve.

When everything is puréed, serve up the soup in bowls, adding a swirl of soya cream to each one and a sprinkling of chives.

CHICORY, CHARD AND CUSTARD CONSOMMÉ

Chicory is a strange and bitter vegetable, generally used raw (if the poor thing's used at all), its leaves acting as little boats for hummus and cream cheese-type things. But there's more to chicory than that. When you fry it in a hot pan, it caramelizes to reveal a sweeter taste. The phyto-chemicals that make it bitter in the first place also make it an excellent tonic for the liver, so eat some to help detoxify yourself in early spring.

There are loads of different types of chicory. They include those creamy white, tight-leafed, rugby ball-shaped Belgian endive buds that you've seen displayed with the lettuces, plus deep red radicchio heads.

Belgian endive is the central star of this chicory consommé, gently supported by the dark green stripes of chard. The potatoes add substance. I've suggested using Remarka or Cara potatoes, which are floury white varieties grown organically in the UK. However, if they're not in season, any other standard-sized floury white potatoes will do.

The steamed custard adds a little protein and a lot of texture, especially if it's made from duck's eggs. The yolks of duck's eggs are more sticky and gelatinous than those of hen's eggs, which makes them much better for making proper homemade custard, as the custard is thicker and generally more substantial. The steamed custard for this soup should be really rubbery, so you can cut it with a knife into little croutony bits to bob around in the soup, adding something to chew on.

The **goat's milk** adds a **creamy background tang**, but, all in all, this is a **subtle soup**.

There's a slight bitterness from the chicory and kuzu, a salty kick from the umeboshi plum seasoning and some fragrance from the dill, but it's the low-key flavour palate of this dish that makes it.

CHICORY, CHARD AND CUSTARD CONSOMMÉ

SERVES 4 AS A STARTER:

FOR THE STEAMED CUSTARD:

2 egg yolks, preferably from duck's eggs

¼ teaspoon herbes de Provence

A pinch of cayenne

A pinch of salt

150ml goat's milk, heated to boiling point

SOUP:

200g Belgian endive (about 4 medium-sized heads)

2 tablespoons olive oil

1 medium onion, peeled and finely chopped

100g Swiss chard, finely sliced

250g Remarka or Cara potatoes, diced into 1cm-ish cubes

1 teaspoon umeboshi plum seasoning

150ml goat's milk

10g kuzu, ground in a suribachi or powdered on the back of a spoon

A handful of chopped dill

Make the steamed custard first. Grease a heatproof bowl or pudding basin. In another bowl, beat the yolks, herbs, cayenne and salt with a fork. Pour the hot goat's milk into the bowl and keep beating. Pour the yolk mixture into your greased bowl and cover it with a small saucepan lid. Suspend the bowl over a small saucepan that's half-full of simmering water, and steam slowly.

Leave the custard to steam on top of the saucepan, over a low heat, for at least 15–20 minutes.

Meanwhile, halve the heads of chicory from top to bottom, then lay each half flat on the board. Slice into strips about 0.5cm wide, then chop the bottom of the leaves off so the strips separate easily.

Heat the oil in a big saucepan, over a medium heat, and throw in the onion when the oil is warm. Fry for a couple minutes, stirring with a wooden spoon, then add the chicory and chard, raising the heat. A minute later, add the potatoes and 1 litre of hot water, lowering the heat to a gentle simmer. Splash in the umeboshi seasoning and cover the pan with a lid. Leave the soup to simmer slowly for 10 minutes, then add the milk with the kuzu dissolved in it. Stir the soup, raising the heat until it's boiling again, and simmer for another few minutes.

The custard should be firm enough to chop by now, so take it off the heat and slice it into little pieces. Put the little eggy bits into four individual bowls, divide the soup between the bowls and scatter some chopped dill over each one.

SUMMER THAI SOUP

This soup is full of the exotic wonders of Seasoned Pioneers spices. Founded by back-packer extraordinaire Mark Steene, this small company provides the most incredible variety of authentic spices from all over the world. I love Mark's spices, because a dish of ingredients that have been locally sourced here in the UK can be utterly transformed, with just a pinch of his magic powders, into a delicious odyssey from the furthest corners of the world. And you can be safe in the knowledge that everything's fairly traded – that he's built proper relationships with the people who grow, roast and blend his wares.

I can see the history of global food reflected in Mark's business. Historians often talk about the spice routes of medieval times, how they influenced different cultures as people found themselves travelling far afield trading spices. However, I believe it was the other way round, and Seasoned Pioneers is my evidence. I think that people were always curious to experience different cultures and started trading spices, and later exotic foods, simply to pay their way. The wanderlust came first and trading was their means to support it. Either way, I'm just happy we can enjoy intense flavours from all over the world, such as the richly stinky kapee shrimp paste, powerful bird's eye chillies, fragrant galangal, sweet lemongrass and delicate kaffir lime leaves that give this Thai soup it's incredibly authentic taste.

SUMMER THAI SOUP

TO SERVE 6 AS A MAIN DISH:

1 kg Joubere (or 1 litre homemade) chicken stock

½ teaspoon kapee shrimp paste

2 teaspoons dried crushed bird's eye chillies

2cm piece fresh ginger root, grated

3 garlic cloves, peeled and grated

1 teaspoon dried lemongrass

4 or 5 pieces of dried shaved galangal

1 level teaspoon black peppercorns

400g uncooked chicken, shredded

4 kaffir lime leaves

2 teaspoons rapadura

400ml coconut milk

1 head of pak choi, finely chopped

2 spring onions, trimmed and finely chopped

100g green beans, topped, tailed and halved

Juice of 1 lime

250g stir-fry rice noodles, broken into 5–8cm pieces

A large handful of fresh coriander, chopped

Heat about 100g (or 100ml) of the chicken stock in a large saucepan until just before boiling point. Break off about half a teaspoon's worth of kapee shrimp paste. Beware! This stuff stinks, as it's basically rotting shrimps. Don't be alarmed though, it'll add gorgeous fishy depths to your soup. Wrap the blob of paste in foil, then hold the little parcel over a flame for a couple of minutes to roast the kapee shrimp paste.

Take the stock off the heat and add the roasted paste, plus the chilli, ginger, garlic, lemongrass, galangal and peppercorns. Leave to steep for 15 minutes, then fish out the galangal, finely chop it with kitchen scissors and throw it back in. Mash the contents of the pan with a fork to make a richly flavoured broth.

Add the chicken, lime leaves and rapadura, then pour in the rest of the stock and the coconut milk. Dark chicken meat from the legs is just as good as breast meat for this dish, if not better, because of its stronger flavour. Simmer gently for half an hour. Throw in the vegetables and lime juice and simmer for 10 more minutes. Add the noodles and the coriander and take the pan off the heat. About 3 minutes later, serve up the soup.

LEEK, SHIITAKE AND MAITAKE SOUP

This creamy opaque soup is a variation of miso, made with sweet, white miso paste. It has sweetness from the miso and caramelized leeks, with saltiness too, all providing a delicate backdrop to the earthy mushroom flavours.

Leeks are special vegetables, full of sweet, earthy, oniony flavours and vitamins B6, E and folate. Shiitake are magnificent mushrooms in terms of health and taste, with cancer-protecting qualities – and they're pretty too. But maitake mushrooms are nothing short of amazing.

The word maitake translates from Japanese as 'dancing mushroom', because people who found them deep in the mountains danced for joy. They were right to do so. Modern research has confirmed maitake are not only one of the most effective natural cancer-curing foods, but that they also support immunity regeneration in people who are HIV positive.

In fact, researchers on one study at the National Cancer Institute in the United States found that maitake extract is as powerful as the anti-AIDS drug AZT, but without its toxic side effects. Maitake are also helpful in controlling cholesterol, aiding the body to get rid of excess fat, supporting steady blood glucose levels in people with diabetes, and even stimulating hair follicles to make your hair grow. If it's these kinds of health-stimulating properties you need, you might want to get hold of some maitake tincture from the supplements bit of the store.

Personally, I eat the dried mushrooms regularly, slipping a few here and there into lots of different dishes. The health properties of maitake mushrooms seem too good to be true, but the facts stand up to scrutiny from scientists who know what they're talking about. I'm sad that so few people seem to know about these tasty little mushrooms that are so full of goodness – so please spread the word. They're not the cheapest ingredients in the world, but with this much going for them, they're a complete bargain. And did I mention that they taste divine?

LEEK, SHIITAKE AND MAITAKE

SOUP

SOUP FOR 2 AS A STARTER:

4g dried maitake mushrooms
1 medium leek
1 tablespoon sunflower oil
1 tablespoon toasted sesame oil
2 garlic cloves, peeled and crushed
4 fresh shiitake mushrooms, sliced
1 teaspoon ground cayenne
1 tablespoon sweet white miso

Soak the maitake in 500ml of warm water for half an hour. Cut the root off
the leek, plus the top of the leaves if they look raggedy. Slice the leek along
its length, lie each half flat on a chopping board, then slice into 1cm-thick
half moon shapes. Put the chopped leek into a colander or sieve and rinse it
under very cold water to wash off any soil. Do it quickly to avoid losing too
much tasty leek juice.

Heat the oils in a medium saucepan, over a medium heat, about
5 minutes before the maitake will be ready to use. Add the leek when the
oil's hot. Fry for a couple of minutes, stirring with a wooden spoon. Add
the garlic, shiitake and cayenne to the pan and keep frying and stirring
for 2 minutes more. Add the maitake and their soaking water and bring

the soup to the boil. Reduce the heat and put the lid on so the soup gently simmers.

Ten minutes later, spoon some of the broth into a ceramic bowl and mix in the miso. Add enough liquid to dissolve the miso, changing it from a paste to a thick liquid. Turn the heat off and pour the diluted miso into the soup. Use some more of the soup liquid to rinse the miso liquor out of the bowl and into the soup. Stir the soup, then dish it up into two bowls.

SALADS

It's kinda hard describing exactly what a salad is.

I mean, the ones involving green things and chopped up vegetables are pretty self-explanatory, but defining why one cold grain is yesterday's rice and another is a salad always stumps me.

So please, just go with this one – **you'll be glad you did**.

LEAFY **SUMMER SALAD**

with Prickly Pear Vinaigrette

A bit of lettuce and tomato is all very well, but why not up the taste factor with a proper mixed leaf salad.

The best mixed salad I have ever eaten was on a family farm in the middle of the New Mexico desert, somewhere near Santa Fe. The people responsible for this delectable salad feast were Howard Yana-Shapiro, the founder of Seeds of Change, and his jeweller wife, Nancy. These friends are deeply committed to growing heirloom varieties of food crops, plus they're veteran hedonists from 1960s San Francisco. The combination means that they grow and prepare the tastiest, greenest, most mixed organic salad ever to be eaten. And they have it near enough every day, plucked fresh from their garden. Inspired, I now cultivate unusual greens in a window box in my London flat, and can promise you it's very easy to do.

There are loads of different lettuces at Fresh & Wild, plenty of special tomatoes and lots of other leafy salad crops. If you do fancy supplementing their lavish range with even more unusual leaves, visit the Seeds of Change online seed collection at Seedsofchange.com and grow your own. Howard is a world-renowned ethno-botanist, so you'll find his organic seeds are astonishingly good in quality and range. Rocket goes crazy on a British balcony, and lambsquarters is a pretty border plant until its day comes to go to the salad bowl in the sky. There are also oodles of strange cucumbers, including the short and round, yellowy-green lemon cucumber.

All the leaves in this recipe are available from Fresh & Wild – assuming you catch them in season – so you can enjoy this very fancy salad without getting grubby fingers, if window boxes and gardens aren't your thing. Once you've got your leaves together, whether by your own fair hand or from Fresh & Wild's greens section, eat them up quick. Organic salad crops have massive advantages over agrochemical salads, as most non-organic lettuces are heavily sprayed with pesticides, and organic leaves have buckets more flavour than agrochemical ones. However, organic salad leaves really don't last long at their best, so dress and serve on the same day you get them if possible, and always keep them in the fridge.

Fresh & Wild have loads of really good ready-made dressings, such as Annie's Naturals Shiitake and Sesame Vinaigrette, and the cutely named Goddess Dressing, plus Tracklements Basil and Balsamic Vinaigrettes. But there's a lot to be said for putting a bunch of your own dressing ingredients into an empty jam jar, then topping it up and shaking every time you want a little bit more. And try adding furikake to this dressing. It's a traditional Japanese sprinkling condiment based around sesame seeds, nori seaweed and red shiso. Furikake comes in many different forms, and Fresh & Wild stock a brand called Sanchi's Vegetarian Furikake. It's usually sprinkled on boiled rice, but I find you can add a bit to almost any savoury dish.

LEAFY **SUMMER SALAD**

with Prickly Pear Vinaigrette

FOR A NICE BIG BOWL OF SALAD, TAKE A FEW LEAVES
FROM A SELECTION OF THE FOLLOWING:

Frisée lettuce

Lolla rossa

Lolla blonda

Red bativa

Green bativa

Red oak leaf lettuce

Green oak leaf lettuce

Red mustard leaves

Green mustard leaves

Baby spinach

Green spray

Mizuna

Ta tsai

Chervil

Konetsuna

Rocket

Coriander

Plus a punnet of gorgeous
   nasturtiums

AND SHAKE THE FOLLOWING INGREDIENTS

IN A JAR FOR THE DRESSING:

2 tablespoons Lunaio extra virgin olive oil infused with lemons

2 tablespoons decent balsamic vinegar

1 tablespoon furikake

1 teaspoon herbes de Provence

1 teaspoon prickly pear honey

A pinch of pepper

It's easy. Just tear all the leaves to the desired size and then toss to mix them up. Don't chop them with a knife, as they'll taste better torn with your hands. Throw the nasturtium flowers on top and drizzle over the dressing immediately before serving. Unbelievable!

RAW ROOTS WITH ORANGE, GINGER AND NUT DRESSING

By now, you're probably pretty clear that I get excited about raw vegetables. So grated raw beetroots and carrots mixed with toasted seeds and then drizzled with a fresh dressing sounds just wonderful, come rain or shine. If you've not tried making a salad like this before, please give it a spin.

Raw roots have many more nutrients in them than cooked ones. Now don't get me wrong, I love my cooked food, and I'm convinced that cooking all kinds of fresh produce is a great thing to do, but most of us need to up the amount of raw foods we eat. This is especially true in winter, when we rely on cooked root vegetables so much more than in abundantly leafy summertime.

One of the main things that all experts agree on is that humans were designed to eat at least five portions of fruit and veg per day. I'm a great believer that at least some of this fruit and veg needs to be eaten raw to gain the maximum benefits. So try eating at least one piece of raw fruit, one piece of raw veg and one salad every day.

It might sound a lot, particularly in winter, but once you start getting into the swing of things, it just becomes normal – especially if you get imaginative with the kinds of fresh produce you can buy.

If you see a weird vegetable, take it home and see what you can do with it. There's bound to be somebody in Fresh & Wild who can suggest what to do with a variety if it's new to you. If it's a vegetable, the chances are you can turn it into a salad – with the exception of tubers, like potatoes, which make great salads when cooked and smothered in mayo, but not, in my opinion, raw. Most other things can be easily dealt with – shredded if it's a salad leaf, chopped if it's a vegetable that grows above the ground or grated if it's a root. You can then add nuts and seeds for added texture and protein, plus fancier things like bean sprouts. And don't forget dressings – once you have a base you can add practically anything else in your cupboard to them.

The basic mix is generally half oil, half acidic liquid, then any other ingredients to be added. These can include honey, dried herbs, tiny cooked brown shrimps, salmon eggs, minced hard-boiled hen's eggs, chopped garlic, crumbled cheese, powdered spices and dried mushrooms. It's all up to your imagination.

Ensure you don't make up too much of this recipe or any other salad, as they're always best eaten fresh on the day you make them. This one goes with practically anything, so start off by trying it in sandwiches. And treat yourself to a decent grater. You can transform dull root crops into light salads quick as a flash if you've got sharp blades. There are loads of cheap but excellent graters around, so try out something a bit more happening than the standard old box grater that's in everyone's cupboards. Thinly shredded carrots somehow taste infinitely subtler than standard grated ones and when you start shredding roots like celeriac, you'll be much happier with the textures you can produce with a finer, sharper grater.

By the way, you'll notice there's a red onion in this salad. You can, of course, simply use a normal brown-skinned onion if you want. Any kind of onion is pretty spectacular, as they all have an incredibly versatile flavour – that's why practically all savoury dishes feature onions. So what's the difference between using brown-skinned ones and red ones? Three things – a milder taste, much less juice and a particularly high concentration of a naturally-occurring phytonutrient called quercetin.

Quercetin is currently being investigated for use in future anti-inflammatory products. However, you can simply slice up some red onions and stick them in a salad to enjoy a plentiful supply of quercetin.

Eat red onions to help soothe eczema, asthma, hay fever, and practically any other allergic sensitivity.

The Seville orange juice featured in this recipe adds an unusual twist to the taste of the dressing. These oranges are only available for a very brief few weeks at the beginning of the year, but you can freeze them whole for later use, as they freeze very well. Seville oranges have a bitter flavour and are almost exclusively used by the British to make marmalade. In fact, nobody gives them a second glance in Seville, probably because they're spoiled with sweet juicy navels – the oranges with the little belly button – and easy-to-peel satsumas and clementines. Of course, you could always go for a Sicilian blood orange if you want, with its sweet juice and blood-red flesh. It depends how sweet you want this salad to be.

RAW ROOTS WITH ORANGE, GINGER AND NUT DRESSING

SALAD FOR 4:

1 medium beetroot

1 medium carrot

¼ of a celeriac

½ a mooli

4 little cherry radishes

1 small turnip

1 medium red onion, peeled and finely chopped

FOR THE DRESSING:

A Seville orange if available or a navel

1 tablespoon olive oil

3 tablespoons hazelnut oil

2 teaspoons toasted sesame seeds

Juice squeezed from 2cm grated ginger root

Scrub all the roots, but don't bother peeling them, apart from the celeriac. Oh what an ugly vegetable, but how full of vitamin C it is. Make sure you get all the knobbly, muddy bits off the celeriac. With the other root veg, cut the fine root tip off and the green leaf stump at the top.

Now grate for England/Wales/Scotland or other country of your choice. Or cheat and whizz the root veg on the grater blade of a food processor.

Put the orange into a bowl of hot water and leave it there for a few minutes. Meanwhile, heat the olive oil in a frying pan, over a medium heat. Take the orange out and slice it open along its middle. Put the open sides down into the oil, being careful not to splash yourself with hot oil. Leave them there for a couple of minutes to caramelize the open fruit and add a rich flavour to the juice.

Now you need to juice the orange. If you've used a Seville orange, you absolutely have to do this with one of the juicing implements available, as they're full of pips and dry of juice, and trying to squeeze it in your hand just won't do the job. A standard old twisty juicer thingy will do – you know, those 1950's-style glass ones (or their Bakelite 1930's predecessors).

Whatever you use, pour the juice into an empty jam jar with all the other dressing ingredients, and shake it, baby. In a big bowl, mix the roots with the onion and dressing, and hey presto – it's ready.

LEAFY **WINTER SALAD**

with Tarragon Mustard and Roasted Onions

It's so easy to just go for stodge in the dark winter months. The gluttony of Christmas followed by the drudge of never-ending chilly nights can leave you reaching for lots of comforting potatoes and meaty stews. Of course, there's nothing wrong with that, but it's essential to balance these warming foods with the freshness and vitality of a really good crunchy salad.

Nature's still big on fresh raw salad options during the winter, especially when you add some home-sprouted seeds. I've invested in a cheap but handy container called The Sprouter which makes home sprouting even easier than the old jam jar method described on page 262. Fresh & Wild have some excellent ready-to-sprout seeds such as the lentil, white radish and fenugreek seed mix. Experiment with your own sprouted seed ideas, too, such as chickpeas, sunflower seeds and the reliable sprouted alfalfa seed.

LEAFY **WINTER SALAD**

with Tarragon Mustard and Roasted Onions

STICK A LARGE BOWL OF THIS SALAD
IN THE CENTRE OF THE TABLE:

Home-sprouted lentil, white radish and fenugreek seeds

¼ of a red cabbage, finely shredded

1 Belgian endive, broken into individual leaves

1 radicchio, coarsely chopped

½ a bunch of watercress, torn into bite-sized pieces

1 big rainbow chard leaf, stalk removed and leaf finely shredded

1 big ruby chard leaf, stalk removed and leaf finely shredded

2 Chinese leaves, shredded

A small head of pak choi, chopped

A stick of celery, de-strung and finely chopped

A handful of curly parsley, finely chopped

FOR THE DRESSING:

1 tablespoon tarragon mustard

Juice of 1 lemon

280g jar of roasted onions, including the oil they're in

2 tablespoons olive oil

Salt and pepper to taste

Toss all the salad ingredients together in a big bowl to thoroughly mix all the flavours. Mix all the dressing ingredients with a fork in another bowl, keeping the lumps of onion intact. Throw the dressing over the salad and toss it all together. Leave for about 10 minutes to allow the flavours to mingle. Serve the salad with bread and cheese for lunch, or as a side dish for a hearty winter dinner.

SEA VEGETABLE SALAD

with Creamy Sweet Dressing

This salad is a winner all year round, especially when served with wholegrain-based dishes or seafood. It's particularly handy if you're running low on fresh land vegetables, as you can keep packets of dried sea veg for months without any loss of nutrients or flavour. It's a good back-up at home, plus a brilliant thing to pack if you're off to some summer festivals. Sea vegetables have strong salty flavours, so a little goes a long way.

Clearspring make a ready-mixed Sea Vegetable Salad that's unique in the UK. It contains wakame and agar with aka tsunomata from the cleanest ocean waters. The combination of translucent, black and deep-red strands is like no other dish I've seen – it's outer planetary food if you ask me. It's great served with this sweet and sour creamy sauce, as the sharpness of the vinegar and rounded sweetness of the syrup brings out the delicate sea vegetable taste.

SEA VEGETABLE SALAD

with Creamy Sweet Dressing

SERVES 4 AS A SIDE DISH:

25g packet Clearspring Sea Vegetable Salad
1 carrot
2 small spring onions

FOR THE DRESSING:
150g fresh tofu
125ml sunflower oil
1 tablespoon toasted sesame oil
3 tablespoons brown rice vinegar
125ml cold water
3 level tablespoons sweet white miso
1 tablespoon brown rice malt syrup
1 tablespoon black or golden sesame seeds

Soak the sea vegetables in hot water for 10 minutes. While they're soaking, scrub the carrot and grate it finely. Top and tail the spring onions, then chop them finely too.

Prepare the dressing by whizzing all the ingredients, except the sesame seeds, in a blender. Toast the seeds in a dry frying pan, on a medium heat, for 2–3 minutes, stirring with a wooden spoon. Pour the dressing into a bowl, mix in the seeds and chill for 10 minutes.

When the sea veg have soaked for 10 minutes, pour off the hot water and rinse the strands under the cold tap for a few seconds. Drain well. Divide equally between four plates, then add a layer of grated carrot to each serving, followed by a layer of spring onion. Pour a quarter of the dressing over each salad and serve.

F & W MOROCCAN COUSCOUS

with Squash and Preserved Lemons

This is a classic Fresh & Wild salad, but again I've adapted it for a home kitchen. It takes a fair bit of preparation. In fact, you need to start doing stuff a month before you eat it! This is all down to the lemons. Throughout the Middle East, people make preserved lemons in their homes to add to dishes, or serve as finger food with olives and pickles. They're really easy to make and pack a mighty, salty, zesty punch.

For the squash in this recipe, see what's in store and choose whichever one tickles your fancy. Hokkaido, buttercup and turban squashes all work really well in this recipe, but feel free to experiment with different kinds of squashes. Most squash fanciers seem to agree that almost all squashes are tastier than the standard orange Hallowe'en pumpkin, so whether it's tiny patty pans or big acorns, try them all out.

Squashes not only taste great but they help the body protect itself from cancer, particularly lung cancer, as they're full of beta-carotene. The seeds are particularly good for male health when washed and roasted as described on page 315.

All in all, it's a top vegetable.

F & W MOROCCAN COUSCOUS

with Squash and Preserved Lemons

TO MAKE 4 PRESERVED LEMONS (YES, FOUR!):

8 lemons
4 tablespoons sea salt

A proper preserving jar is best for preparing the lemons. These are the jars with a rubber ring to seal the top, like a fancy beer bottle. If you have one, sterilize it by steeping it in boiling water along with its lid and rubber seal. If not, sterilize a couple of big jam jars and their lids in boiling water.

Using a sharp knife, cut four of the lemons down to the central core, but not through it. Keep the lemons from falling apart whilst making the deepest channels you can. Squeeze as much salt as you can into these cuts, then put the lemons into the sterilized jar, packing them as tightly as you can. Throw in any salt that's left over and seal the lid tightly. Three days later, open up the jar and add the juice of the other four lemons. Close it again tightly and put it in a cold and dark place such as a basement, larder cupboard or the back of a shed – and don't forget where you've put it. A month later you'll have perfectly preserved lemons.

FOR 6 SIDE SERVINGS OF COUSCOUS:

3 tablespoons sunflower oil
1 tablespoon sesame oil

500g couscous

3 teaspoons Marigold bouillon of your choice

500g squash, cubed, seeds discarded

1 tablespoon tamari

3cm piece ginger root, grated

2 medium onions, peeled and chopped

25g sesame seeds

125g dried apricots, soaked in hot water

A big handful of fresh coriander

A big handful of fresh mint

20 Kalamata olives

1 preserved lemon, finely chopped

Extra fresh mint to taste (optional)

Set the oven to 200°C/400°F/Gas Mark 6. Heat the sunflower and sesame oils in a roasting tin for a few minutes. Prepare the couscous by mixing the bouillon powder into 1 litre of boiling water and pouring this stock over the grain. Cover the bowl and leave it to cool.

Add the squash, tamari, ginger, onion and sesame seeds to the hot oil in the roasting tin. Roast for about half an hour, then take the tin out of the oven and stir the vegetables with a wooden spoon. If the squash seems soft inside and the onions have cooked and caramelized, keep the tin out of the oven. If not, continue roasting the veg for 10 more minutes.

When the vegetables are ready, fluff up the couscous with a fork and spoon. Coarsely chop the apricots and herbs. Mix them into the couscous with the roasted mixture and the olives.

Add some of the chopped lemon, mix it in and taste the salad. If you think it should be saltier, add more preserved lemon to taste. And, if you like it herby, now's your chance to add some more fresh mint for a more tabbouleh-style, deeply herbal experience.

F & W RED CAMARGUE RICE

with Cashew Nuts and Green Beans

If you're one of the many people who visit Fresh & Wild for your daily lunch, you'll know and love this chewy red rice salad. But how about your family and friends? Treat them to it as a weekend lunch, with a selection of sliced cold meats and deli fish, such as Islay's smoked beef in single malt Scotch whisky, chorizo, lomo embuchado and ham, plus marinated or rollmop herrings and sustainably-caught tinned sardines. It's good cold as a side dish with chicken and pulse dishes, but I must admit, I much prefer it hot.

There are two kinds of red rice available in store, but I use the variety that comes from the Camargue in Southern France for this dish. It's grown by the Griotto family, near the warm Mediterranean coast, and is full of sunshine goodness. The current Mr Griotto's father noticed that a few grains from his standard short grain rice crop had naturally mutated to become an attractive deep red. He then grew a starter crop of seeds from these first accidental red rice grains, and from this the current Camargue red rice crops grew. So it's pretty special stuff, being a very modern crop made exclusively along organic lines. And the chewy texture and delicate flavour has made it the gourmet choice of chefs and connoisseurs the world over.

F & W RED CAMARGUE RICE

with Cashew Nuts and Green Beans

MAKES ENOUGH FOR 6 AS A SIDE DISH:

150g red Camargue rice

75g brown short grain rice

3 sticks celery, thinly sliced

1 medium leek, stripped of its outer leaf, topped, tailed and thinly sliced

2 tablespoons sunflower frying oil

1 tablespoon toasted sesame oil

6 medium garlic cloves, peeled and grated

6cm piece ginger root, grated

2 tablespoons ground cayenne

Juice of ¼ a lemon

1¼ tablespoons brown rice vinegar

1¼ tablespoons tamari

200g mushrooms, halved

130g French beans, topped, tailed and cut in half

A handful of freshly chopped parsley

90g toasted cashew nut pieces

Sea salt to taste

Cook the red rice in a saucepan with 350ml of water and cook the brown rice in a separate pan in 250ml of water. Simmer them both for about 40 minutes, or until the water has been absorbed.

In a large frying pan, fry the celery and leek, in the oils, over a medium heat. After a few minutes, add the garlic, ginger, cayenne, lemon juice, vinegar and tamari, and stir well. Add the mushrooms and beans and cook for 5 minutes with the lid on. The beans should still be a bit crunchy. Mix the veg with the boiled rices, the parsley and the cashews. Add a little salt to taste and either leave to cool or serve straight away whilst it's still warm.

F & W BALSAMIC BEETS

Beets are the punks of the root family. From the way they turn your fingers pink to their earthy sweetness, beetroots rock. I don't understand why everyone seems to only eat the ready-cooked beetroot you get in plastic packs. Although they're undeniably nice served like that, they're infinitely more versatile when bought raw, either for cooking at home or serving raw in a salad. The solid crew of beets in this recipe is so tasty I'm pretty sure you'll start slipping them into lots more dishes.

In addition to being strong on flavour, beetroot has pretty impressive health credentials. For a start, it helps the cells in your body absorb oxygen from your blood better. Given that people are starting to go to oxygen bars to breathe canisters of pure O_2, maybe we ought to be simply eating more beets and drinking more beetroot juice.

When your body's cells are able to take in more oxygen, a myriad of health opportunities become possible. There's the possibility of improved immunity, better brain function and an improvement in certain anaemic conditions.

Beetroot's been used as a **general pick-me-up** for centuries.

It's great for your digestive system, cleansing everything from your liver to your bowel on its way through. And it's been used all over Eastern Europe as a general tonic and blood cleanser for as long as anyone can remember, mostly in the form of a piping hot bowl of borscht.

There's now also a lot of evidence building that suggests beetroot could play a key role in preventing, treating and even curing some kinds of cancers, if used effectively. (For more information about this work, visit the Bristol Cancer Help Centre's website, listed in the resources section.)

But back to this salad. If you're lucky, your beetroots may come with their tops intact, ready to provide a lovely leafy side salad. Either way, you can't go wrong with this punchy, crunchy salad. It's good served hot if you can't wait to tuck in, but it also keeps in the fridge for three or four days. So if you're skiving work, you can still enjoy a proper Fresh & Wild lunchtime treat. Oh, and don some Marigolds if you want to preserve your manicure.

F & W BALSAMIC BEETS

2kg raw beetroots, scrubbed
3 tablespoons olive oil
100ml balsamic vinegar
Salt and crushed black pepper to taste
1 tablespoon concentrated apple juice
2 handfuls freshly chopped flat-leaf parsley

Turn your oven on to 200°C/400°F/Gas Mark 6. As with most organic veg, don't bother peeling your beets. Instead, top and tail them, cut in half from top to bottom, in half again and then into thirds to make 2cm-ish cubes. Put them into two big turkey-roasting tins and pour the oil and vinegar over the top. Sprinkle over salt and pepper to taste, roll the beets about in the liquid, then cover with foil. Roast for about 45 minutes.

Take the tray out, remove the foil and stir the beetroot. Put it back in the oven without the foil for another 15 minutes. Now add the apple juice concentrate to the liquid and stir in well to dissolve. Make sure all the beet pieces are coated well. Either leave to cool or serve hot, sprinkled with the parsley.

F & W BARLEY SALAD

with Hazelnuts

Next time you're in the shop, have a good look at all the dried grains. Everyone seems to just grab a packet of rice and then run to the chocolate section, but there are so many other grains to explore. All whole grains are packed with goodness. This means stacks of B complex vitamins that help you deal with the stresses and strains of modern life, plus loads of trace minerals.

Barley, however, has additional strengths because of its high content of something called beta glucans. Scientific research in the USA has found that these compounds slow down the rate at which your liver makes cholesterol. Although medieval peasants obviously weren't aware that this is the case, they ate barley like there was no tomorrow. Herbalists throughout the centuries have given women barley water to sooth cystitis and everyone else barley water to ease constipation.

Fresh & Wild sell two different kinds of barley, pearl and pot. Pot barley is just the grain with the outer husk removed. Pearl barley is the same thing, but has been refined more by grinding the outside, so it cooks quicker. Pot barley has more fibre and nutrition, as much of any grain's goodness is in the outer part. That said, they're both high-fibre foods that are full of good carbohydrates and vitamins – and that distinctive barley flavour that's so reminiscent of Eastern Europe. If you're new to barley, start with the pearl variety, as it's lighter. If you know you like barley, go for pot barley grain, as it's got more of the chewy texture and earthy flavour that you'll love.

Why not try this salad from Fresh & Wild's lunch counter, then give it a go if you're hooked on barley's mellow flavour? You'll also find barley couscous in the same dried goods section and this makes a lovely Moroccan Couscous with Pumpkin and Preserved Lemons (see page 225). And try barley semolina, as used in the breakfast Gamut of Kamut® recipe on page 30.

This recipe makes a delicious warm salad. To eat it cold, wait for the barley and leeks to reach room temperature before pouring on the dressing.

F & W BARLEY SALAD

with Hazelnuts

TO SERVE 5 AS A SIDE DISH:

250g pot or pearl barley

100g chopped hazelnuts or cobnuts when they're in season

500g leeks, trimmed, outer leaves removed and finely sliced

A pinch of ground cayenne

3cm piece ginger root, grated

3 garlic cloves, peeled and grated

100ml olive oil

2 tablespoons brown rice vinegar

1¼ tablespoons tamari

1 tablespoon apple juice concentrate

1 teaspoon coarse-grain mustard

A handful of freshly chopped curly parsley

A pinch of sea salt and black pepper

First, rinse the barley well, then bring it to the boil in 750ml of water. Reduce the heat to a simmer and cook, with the lid on, for about an hour and a half. Check regularly to see if it needs more water, as it mustn't run dry.

About 10 minutes before the barley's done, put the hazelnuts on a baking tray and roast them in the oven at 200°C/400°F/Gas Mark 6. Fry the leeks, cayenne, ginger and garlic in the olive oil, over a medium heat, taking them off the heat before they go mushy.

Drain the excess water off the barley, if there is any, then mix the nuts and the leek mixture into the grain. In a cup, whisk the vinegar, tamari, apple juice concentrate, mustard and parsley with a fork, plus a bit of salt and pepper to taste. Toss the salad in the dressing just before serving.

BREADS & SPREADS

Clive Wells
Hobbs House Bakery, Chipping Sodbury, Gloucestershire

'Our miller's slow but sure process encapsulates everything we believe in. Here, nothing is rushed, nothing is hurried. It's all about quality, character and flavour, and time-honoured, trusted artisan processes.'

BREADS

Get involved with your bread. Squidge that dough.

Try out fresh yeast from the fridge, a forgotten commodity in these days of easy-blend dried sachets. Make enough fresh bread-baking smells to make people long to buy your house as they wander past the door, even though it's not for sale. Here are eight easy breads for you to try. There's nothing tricky about them and everything special about them.

I've included modern inventions, an ancient loaf, some worldwide dailies, strange breadsticks and a sweet, cakey number.

PHAT GREEN FLAT BREAD

If you like the taste of fresh greens, you'll love this easy bread recipe. Unlike most herby breads, this one won't work unless you have handfuls of fresh herbs or fresh salad greens. I've used parsley and coriander but you can try it with mint or basil. Alternatively, for extra bite and a touch of bitterness, use watercress, or for a more subtle taste and colour, use alfalfa sprouts.

Don't be fooled by the name. This bread isn't green – it's brown with little green speckledy bits. And it isn't flat – more flying saucer shaped. But it's totally phat.

PHAT GREEN FLAT BREAD

25g fresh yeast

1 teaspoon rapadura

3 tablespoons lukewarm whole milk

250g strong wholemeal bread flour, plus a bit more to sprinkle

¼ teaspoon salt

20g fresh parsley, finely chopped

20g fresh coriander, finely chopped

3 tablespoons plain yogurt, at room temperature

75ml lukewarm water

In a mixing bowl, cream together the yeast and rapadura to make a paste. Stir in the milk, then sprinkle on about a tablespoon of flour. Leave it in a warm part of your kitchen for about 10 minutes. It should be properly frothy when you come back to it.

Stick the flour and salt in a big bowl, then stir in the parsley and coriander. Mix in the yeast mixture and yogurt when the 10 minutes are up, using clean hands. Scrunch the mixture some more, adding the water bit by bit to form a soft 'n' sticky dough. You might not need to use all the water, depending on how the flour's feeling today, so see how your particular dough goes.

When you have a sticky, soft dough, flour your work surface and turn the dough out of the bowl and onto the floured patch. Sprinkle some flour onto your fingers and knead the dough for 5–10 minutes, until the dough stops being so sticky and starts being more dough-ish.

At this point, put it into a lightly oiled bowl, stick a carrier bag around the bowl and bung it in your airing cupboard for about an hour. When it comes out again, flour the surface again, then knock the dough back by lightly kneading it for about one minute. Shape it into a ball and put the ball of dough onto a baking tray. Finally, flatten it into a circle about 2cm thick, then stick the tray with the dough back into the carrier bag, then back into the airing cupboard for another 45 minutes.

When it's been in the airing cupboard for about half an hour, turn your oven on to 220°C/425°F/Gas Mark 7. It'll take a good 10–15 minutes to get truly scorching in there. If you like your bread soft, brush some olive oil over the dough after it's finished rising, but before you put it into the oven. When the dough's rising time is up and the oven's baking hot, put the tray (minus the carrier bag) into the middle of the oven.

Bake it for about 15 minutes, until it forms a nice crunchy crust and goes 'brown bread' brown. Leave it to cool, then serve with almost anything savoury, from artisan cheeses like Irish Cashel Blue and French Brie de Meaux, to salads, dinners and spreads.

BOOZY BEER BREAD

At the turn of the eighteenth century, this recipe would have got me thrown into prison in Paris – or in prohibition America in the 1920s, for that matter. In the case of France it wouldn't be because it was a 'dry' state – no, that's never been likely. It would have been because of its harmful influence on our morals. Let me explain.

Most cultures have connected what they eat with who they are, from the medicinal dietary beliefs of ancient Greece to the spiritual dietary laws of modern Islam. France has its own deep historical beliefs based around all kinds of food, but particularly around bread.

In seventeenth century France, light white breads like croissants and brioche were for the urban rich, while heavy wholemeal sourdough was for the rural peasants. This dietary segregation wasn't purely due to monetary considerations, although refined flours and baking expertise did put the Parisian bakers' light white breads out of the league of most peasants in terms of cost. The driving force behind the division was a belief that bread was somehow connected to moral fibre and good old-fashioned work ethics.

The French Catholic church and ruling aristocracy – which was basically the same thing in those pre-Napoleon days – believed that the bread people ate defined their morality. Traditional sourdough (which is completely delicious) is made using a little bit of sourdough dough kept aside from the loaf before. Light, white breads are made with yeast, which was always a by-product of the Belgian beer industry in France during that period. So whilst the sourdough had a direct lineage way back to generations of decent French breads, the white breads simply had some foreign beer muck added to make them rise – shock, horror!

The ruling classes genuinely believed that if the peasants ate white breads made with Belgian yeast, they'd watch their hard-working nationalistic subjects become slovenly good-for-nothings. Hence the gravity of the famous call to 'Let them eat cake'.

The long, hard kneading process involved in making sourdough was also believed, by those with a vested interest, to make French peasants resilient and strong. And the fact that the yeast for white bread came from beer instead of wine, the French tipple of choice, meant that the peasants were even more likely to revolt – which of course they did in 1789, having had enough of silly ideas about whether they were allowed to eat brioche or not.

There's plenty to be said for the good old-fashioned ale used in this naughty, yeast-risen bread. For a start, it provides real flavour. Really great organic beers are brewed from full-flavoured, heirloom ingredients – and they're brewed by real people, not by big factories. And the people involved in organic brewing simply love what they do.

Take Peter Scholey, the guy who's won the Champion Organic Beer of Britain award more times then anybody else. He loves organic beer. The main reasons he rates organic over non-organic beer are the quality of organic hops and the skills of the makers. The effort involved in producing organic beer means that the people who make them are guaranteed enthusiasts. There is currently not much financial incentive to brew organic, so those that do it must care more about what they are doing. And that shows in the quality of what they produce.

Also, organically grown **hops** tend to **taste stronger and better**.

Peter thinks they look more raggedy because they're harder to grow, but believes it's this adversity that makes them more flavourful, like grapes grown on difficult terrain.

Of course, organic smallholdings often grow heirloom crops. With beers, this means old-fashioned varieties of barley, such as Plumage Archer, and traditional vintage Kentish hops, like First Gold. And with various innocuous but corner-cutting additives banned under organic guidelines, brewers resort to traditional flavour-building techniques. The easy caramel option isn't available to organic brewers, so organic brewers use roasted barley syrup instead, a much nicer tasting ingredient.

Strange as it may seem, proper beers have recently been pinpointed as having a number of positive health benefits. They're thought to help stop people developing osteoporosis and gall and kidney stones. Plus there's research going on to see how beers can prevent Type 2 diabetes mellitus and even senile dementia.

So make sure you choose organic ale to make this recipe, and then settle down to a ploughman's lunch with some artisan-made cheddar, a lovely traditional pickle and a glass of organic ale.

As for the hemp seeds sprinkled on this loaf, they add a lovely nutty crunchy texture to the crispy crust. Hemp is one of the most awesome crops that people can grow. It's an invaluable crop for organic farmers, particularly farmers needing to build their soil's nutritional quality, because hemp is one of the only crops that actually nourishes the soil with more nutrition than it draws out.

In terms of human health, hemp has a more balanced and complete protein profile than any other crop, soya beans included, and comes in a particularly digestible form. It also has the most suitable fatty acid balance of any oil currently known, and is really helpful in relieving PMS, eczema (when eaten or applied) and some joint problems, such as arthritis.

Of course, a few seeds won't do wonders for you, but start integrating hemp products into your general diet. Look out for hemp oil for salad dressings, hemp flours and pastas, and even hemp cheeses. In fact, hemp can be made into practically anything, which is why environmentalists are so up for it – from making it into renewable plastics to using it in soaps and beauty products. And of course, it was the original fibre used to make denim.

Food for thought ...

BOOZY BEER BREAD

500g strong white bread flour
2 teaspoons baking powder
1 tablespoon dried dill
1 teaspoon salt
About 350ml strong ale
4 small spring onions, trimmed and finely chopped
50g Montgomery Cheddar cheese, grated
A little milk
2 tablespoons hemp seeds

Turn the oven on to 190°C/375°F/Gas Mark 5. Mix the flour, baking powder, dill and salt in a big mixing bowl. Add the beer, little by little, stirring with your hands until there's enough beer in there to form a soft dough. Throw in the spring onions and cheese and knead the dough, adding a bit more flour if the mixture is too sticky. Sprinkle some flour onto a work surface, plonk the dough on top, shape it into a round ball and then flatten it into a loaf shape about 20cm in diameter.

Paint the top with milk using a brush, if you have one, or your fingers if you don't. Press the hemp seeds onto the milk lightly, then put the loaf on a well-oiled baking sheet. Bake the bread for about 40–45mins. It's ready when it's golden brown, smells heavenly and makes a hollow sound when you tap it. Leave the loaf to cool thoroughly, then tear off big chunks and top it with your favourite cheese. St Tola organic Irish goat's cheese is particularly good with it.

CUMIN CHAPATIS

Nothing complements a North Indian meal better than chapatis. They're one of the easiest breads to make at home, as proven by millions of people every day. Chapatis are generally served plain, but these ones are a bit fancy because of the cumin. Plain or spiced, chapatis are a staple bread, and so simple to make.

FOR A DOZEN CHAPATIS:

185g strong wholemeal bread flour
1 tablespoon whole black cumin seeds
1 tablespoon sunflower oil
1 teaspoon salt
150ml warm water
A pot of ghee to serve

In a bowl, mix all the ingredients using your hands. Add a bit more warm water if the dough seems too dry. You're after a firm dough consistency, but it obviously needs to have enough water to stick together. Flour a work surface, then knead the dough on it for a few minutes. Put the dough in a clean plastic carrier bag and leave it for between 30 minutes and two hours. The longer you leave it, the better the chapatis.

When it's time to roll the chapatis, first knead the dough for another few minutes. Divide the dough into 12 even-sized pieces and roll them into balls. Heat a heavy iron pan or a frying pan on a low heat. Meanwhile, roll out the balls of dough into thin 10cm circles.

When the pan is hot, put the first circle of dough into it. After a few minutes, check the side that's touching the pan. If it's going brown and there's a mouth-watering cooked-dough smell, flip the chapati. When both sides are done, take the chapati out of the pan and put the next one in. If dark spots are appearing on the bread, turn down the heat.

Meanwhile, if you have a gas flame on your hob, hold the cooked chapati over it for a few seconds using a pair of tongs so you don't burn yourself. This will make it go puffy. While they're still hot, spread the chapatis with a thin layer of ghee.

CARIBE CHILLI TORTILLAS

Proper tortillas start with dried kernels of white Mexican corn, and involve hours of laborious pounding, kneading and preparation. Cheat's tortillas take minutes.

These wheat-based tortillas are flavoured with sweet, crushed caribe chillies. Contrary to popular belief in Britain, chillies come in all sorts of flavours and heats. In most chilli-friendly cuisines, people have specific favourite varieties for different dishes, and rightly so. The flavours vary considerably, from smoky through to fruity tones, and there's a million zillion degrees of fire between cayenne and Bolivian black chillies.

Caribe chillies are fairly mild in terms of heat, but are a particularly lush and highly flavoured variety from Mexico, the **home of the tortilla**.

If you like your chillies hotter, go for crushed pasillas instead. But if you do up the heat, serve with a bowl of yogurt on the side.

CARIBE CHILLI TORTILLAS

TO MAKE A DOZEN TORTILLAS:

500g wholemeal flour
1 tablespoon baking powder
1 teaspoon salt
1 tablespoon crushed caribe chilli flakes
2 tablespoons butter
About 300ml warm water

Mix the flour, baking powder, salt and chillies in a big bowl. Rub in the butter so that it's evenly mixed, then add the water bit by bit, mixing it in with your fingers. You may not need all the water – what you're after is a soft dough that isn't too sticky, so stop adding water when it reaches this consistency. Flour your work surface, then knead the dough for about 5 minutes.

Divide the dough into 12 equal-sized pieces, then roll each ball into a circle as thin as it will go without breaking – this will be about 20–23cm wide and less than a millimetre thick.

Heat a small frying pan over a medium heat, then cook the tortillas, one at a time, on both sides, until they're golden brown. This shouldn't take more than about 2–3 minutes per side, as the tortillas need to stay flexible enough to be used as wraps. They will puff up a bit and smell ready when it's time to take them off the heat. Stack the tortillas on a plate and cover them with a clean tea towel to keep them warm. Once you've finished frying all the tortillas, fill them with anything from avocados to roasted beef (see the lunch recipe on page 63).

QUINOA GRISSINI

Quinoa (pronounced *keen-wah*) was the staple grain of Peru for millennia, until the arrival of the conquistadors brought the widespread use of white rice, which was a great shame, as quinoa has a lot more going for it in lots of ways. It's much higher in protein, has a more balanced nutritional profile and the whole grain cooks in half the time of whole grain rice. What's more, if you add quinoa grain into soups and stews, they turn into tiny spirals – try it, it'll add a touch of magic to your lunch.

As for these grissini, they're simple and quick to mix and bake, delivering crunchy Peruvian dippers ready to plunge into hummus, get smothered with soft santola goat's cheese, or have strips of roll-mop herrings wrapped around them.

QUINOA GRISSINI

FOR A DOZEN GRISSINI:

1 teaspoon rapadura
15g fresh yeast
100ml lukewarm water
100g wholemeal flour
75g quinoa flour
1 teaspoon sesame seeds
1 tablespoon soy milk
1 tablespoon olive oil
A pinch of sea salt

In a large bowl, cream the rapadura (unrefined sugar) and yeast together, stir in the water and sprinkle over a tablespoon of the flour. Leave the mixture for about 10–15 minutes, until properly frothy. Add everything else and thoroughly mix with your hands. When everything's combined, keep kneading for about 5 minutes. Put the ball of dough into an oiled bowl, put the bowl into a plastic carrier bag and put the bag into your airing cupboard. Go and do something else for an hour. Take it out an hour later and throw the dough onto a floured surface.

Turn your oven on to 200°C/400°F/Gas Mark 6. Slice the dough with a sharp knife into twelve equal-sized pieces, then roll them into very thin sausages about 30cm long. Take two floured baking trays and put six grissini on each, leaving a 5cm gap between them. Slide the trays into plastic carrier bags, then leave the bread to rise for another quarter of an hour. Remove the trays and bake for 15–20 minutes. Push the sticks about to make sure they're not stuck to the tray, then leave to cool.

CARAWAY POTATO BAGELS

This is the stodgiest, stickiest bread recipe in the galaxy, but somehow it's made with gluten-free potato flour. I didn't believe that such a thing was possible until recently.

The answer lies in an ingenious product called xanthan gum powder, which you'll find stationed just by the flours and cake flavourings. It's made from corn syrup that's been fermented with a micro-culture, sort of like yogurt making. The result is a dry, white, high-fibre powder with a strong gelling capability. And it's the secret ingredient essential to gluten-free baking success.

You can easily use other gluten-free flours in this recipe, opening up the world of bagel enjoyment to non-wheat-eaters. Try, for example, using gram, brown rice and chestnut flours, or maize meal. And play around with different flavourings, like diced, pre-baked onions or minced capers. For perfect results, all you have to remember is to keep the relative amounts of xanthan gum powder and gluten-free flour the same. And if you fancy making homemade bagels that do contain wheat flour, go ahead with this same method, but leave out the gum.

CARAWAY POTATO BAGELS

500g potato flour

1¼ teaspoons xanthan gum powder

1 teaspoon salt

25g fresh yeast

1 tablespoon rapadura

2 tablespoons soft butter

2 tablespoons caraway seeds (optional)

300ml soy milk

1 egg yolk, lightly beaten

Put the flour in a big bowl and thoroughly mix in the xanthan powder and salt. In another bowl, mash the yeast with half the rapadura. Heat the butter in a saucepan, over a low heat, and throw in the caraway seeds, if you're using them, when the butter's melted. Jiggle the saucepan over the heat to keep the seeds moving, then add the milk and the rest of the rapadura. Dip a clean finger in after a minute, to see if the milk mix is lukewarm yet. When it is, take the pan off the heat and pour the liquid into the yeast mixture to dissolve the yeast. Watch it bubble for a couple of minutes, then pour the beaten egg yolk and the warm milk into the flour bowl.

Mix everything with your hands to make a strangely soft dough. Knead it well for about 10 minutes, until it's quite firm. Cover the bowl with a damp tea towel and leave it in the airing cupboard for about an hour. Flour your work surface, and put the dough in the middle of it. Knead it for another 10–15 minutes, until you can knead no more.

Now make sausages from small pieces of dough, rolling them until they're about 10–15cm long and as thin as your thumb. When all your sausages are lined up, turn them all into rings, sticking the ends together with a drop of water. Leave them to rise on the floured surface for about 10 minutes.

Meanwhile, turn your oven on to 200°C/400°F/Gas Mark 6. Heat a big saucepan half-filled with water on a low to medium heat until it's simmering, and grease some baking trays. When the bagels have rested for 10 minutes, gently lower them, one by one, into the hot water using a fish slice. Don't forget that they'll rise and expand as they boil, so only add a couple of bagels at a time to the water. Keep gently simmering for about 2 minutes. Fish each one out with the fish slice and lay them onto the baking trays.

When they've all been boiled, put them into the oven and bake for about 20–25 minutes. They're done when they're golden brown and crisp on the outside. Potato bagels are best eaten on the day you make them. You can cut them in half and butter them straight away, or leave them to cool down before freezing for another day.

ESSENE BREAD

My pal Kate Wood is a mother of three and her whole family eats raw vegan food about 80 per cent of the time.

Hence Kate's version of this ancient recipe is uncooked, but heated in a dehydrator machine. However, I've adapted it so it can be slow-cooked in a normal gas or electric oven. It's bursting with nutrition, as it's still near enough raw, and has a dense, chewy texture. It's very very sweet and moist like a malt loaf, but has absolutely no added sugar. Instead, there are loads of dates and raisins to keep it sweet. This is definitely not the kind of bread you can slice and butter, but more the kind you pull chunks off and chew.

The original Essene bread was made around two thousand years ago by the Essene people, a Jewish sect based in ancient Palestine. These guys saw food as a sacred living thing and expertly harnessed food's healing abilities. Of course, they hadn't yet discovered modern culinary techniques and this is reflected in the bread. It's deeply wholefoody, the heaviest, densest, sweetest bread you can imagine – and it's gorgeously sticky and chewy with it.

It's a scientific fact that a sprouted seed has twelve times the original nutritional value of the seed before germination. The Essene people knew this instinctively, because it's obvious to people living close to nature as they did. A seed is gearing up to become a big plant when it first sprouts, so it utilizes all its strength. If you munch it at this stage, there are some pretty major benefits to be enjoyed. They'd make their bread by sprouting grain, crushing it between rocks, then baking it in the sunshine.

Sadly, this method doesn't work on the balcony of my London flat, so I've provided this oven method instead for your delectation. The heat setting on the oven is so low that you can't really say that it's baked as such, especially as most commercially-available Essene bread is baked in short blasts of very hot heat. I'm happier with my slowly-does-it method, as it doesn't destroy the lovely nutrients, but still makes the loaf gel together nicely. It's very close to the ancient sun-baked version, especially if you use ancient grains like spelt instead of modern wheat grain.

This recipe does take some planning because before you can make it, **you have to sprout the grain**, which takes about five days.

First, choose which grain you're going to use. All are delicious and very good for you, and all of them will make a fairly sweet loaf as the complex starches gently break down into sugars.

You can sprout grain in shallow bowls, or in the wonderfully named Bio Snacky Mini Greenhouse Germinator, which you'll find in some of the stores. It's a small glass stacked tray thingummy that makes the tending of your grains that little bit easier.

Either way, it's a particularly nice thing to do if there are kids around, as they love getting involved with growing things. Seeing the grain berries sprout is exciting stuff when you're little, especially when you can get involved with making the final loaf. To be honest, it's pretty exciting stuff when you're an adult and it still gets me secretly excited as I watch them grow.

And if you're trying to get pregnant, how about checking this out for a giggle. Wee on some grain in a dish that you don't intend to ever eat out of again. Get your partner to do the same in another disposable dish. If your grain sprouts a lot quicker than your partner's grain, chances are you've got a bun in the oven. Foul but true.

But back to the culinary task at hand. Once your Essene bread is cooked, pull chunks off and eat it just like that, or spread it with pumpkin seed, almond, cashew or hazelnut butters for a rich teatime treat.

ESSENE BREAD

FOR ONE SMALL LOAF:

150g rye, spelt, kamut®, or buckwheat grain

125g dates

125g raisins

2 tablespoons Brazil nuts

2 tablespoons sesame seeds

2 tablespoons pumpkin seeds

2 tablespoons ground cinnamon

Soak the grain of your choice overnight in cold water, then drain the water the next day. After that, rinse with cold water once every morning and once every night for three to four days. Not a lot will happen for the first few days, but they'll suddenly go wild on about day three. The grain will double in size, sprouting wiggly roots and sprouts. If you try a raw sprouted seed, you'll taste their subtle sweetness.

You'll need to make the bread on the fourth or fifth day, as this is when the sprouts are at their best.

Put the little sprouts and everything else in a food processor in small batches and whizz until it all comes together into a sticky dough. Don't put all the sprouts in at the same time, or you'll risk straining the motor on your food processor. On a floured worktop, shape the dough into a long, fat sausage. Don't make a classic loaf shape, as the gentle heat used wouldn't touch the centre of this sort of loaf. Oil a baking sheet and put your loaf on it.

Just before bedtime, set your oven to 50°C/100°F or, if you have a gas cooker, lower than Gas Mark 1/4. Basically, set your oven as low as it will go and put your bread in. In the morning, your Essene bread will be done. I recommend a minimum of 8 hours beauty sleep for a perfect loaf and up to 12 hours if you'd like it fairly firm.

Alternatively, make an oval loaf shape with the dough, and bake it for 2–3 hours at 100°C/200°F/Gas Mark 1/4. This will make a firmer loaf whilst still retaining lots of the nutrients and enzymes in the sprouts.

SWEET ORANGE NUT BREAD

Polenta is an Italian maize ingredient that's useful in baking or simply cooked into a porridge. I was lucky enough to eat an amazing savoury polenta dish in Venice last year, cooked by Californian chef and food activist Alice Waters. She'd slow-cooked the polenta porridge for hours and served it with a traditional stewed pork. Eaten with new friends and good friends, the meal was one of those totally special dinners that I'll never forget. If you're ever in Berkeley, California, go visit her restaurant Chez Panisse.

Alice is a supporter of good, proper food, particularly organic and slow food. As well as running her acclaimed restaurant, she's the force behind a project called The Edible Schoolyard. The aim is for every school in America to create a vegetable garden, so the kids can plant food and then learn to cook the produce they grow.

'We're told that cooking is drudgery, that it's easier to just buy cheap, prepared food,' said Alice recently. 'Drink cola and eat hamburgers. Billions are spent convincing us, it washes over us constantly. It's not surprising that people buy into it and get addicted to junk food.'

When children make the connection between the food they grow in school and the food they usually eat, they naturally get excited about eating good food instead of junk food. In fact, this principle works for adults, too. Try growing a few herbs in a window box and you'll soon see that you can't wait to eat them.

When we make a connection with the food that we eat, we start to make wider connections, beyond the enjoyment of food and nature – observations about society, about how things work and connect. All in all, the Edible Schoolyard programme is brilliant – I wonder if anyone will emulate the idea here in the UK? Now there's something to chew on ...

This bread is very cakey, so serve it at teatime or for **a special weekend breakfast.**

I usually just eat it plain, but it also goes well with subtly flavoured creamy cheeses or Kooky Aduki (see page 291).

SWEET ORANGE NUT BREAD

MAKES ONE 20CM X 10CM LOAF:

60g–75g rapadura, depending on how sweet your tooth is

90g walnut pieces

80g soft butter

4 large eggs

50g polenta

50g strong wholemeal bread flour

1 tablespoon cornflour

1 heaped teaspoon baking powder

Zest and juice of 1 orange

Toasted sesame seeds

Heat the oven to 160°C/325°F/Gas Mark 3. Put the rapadura and walnuts in a blender and whizz until smooth. Cream the butter in a food processor until it's fluffy, then add the walnut mixture slowly, continuing to whizz the butter as it joins it in the bowl. Add the eggs one at a time with the motor still running.

Mix the polenta, flour, cornflour and baking powder in another bowl. Beat this mixture into the creamy mixture, mixing well with a wooden spoon. Add the juice and zest and stir well.

Pour the batter into a well-greased 20cm x 10cm loaf tin and sprinkle the sesame seeds on top. Bake for about 40 minutes, until a metal knife, inserted into the centre of the bread, comes out clean. Take the bread out of the oven, but keep it in the tin for a good 15 minutes before turning it out onto a cooling rack.

SPREADS

Hummus again? Cheese on toast?

Yes please, they're both completely lovely – but not all the time! There's a world of possibilities out there; a plethora of ingredients eager to get in your basket and tantalize your tongue.

Let them. Just let them.

ZAHTAR STARTER

This recipe is basically a guacamole that shuns its Central American roots and instead thinks it's from the Middle East. Not content with the usual lemony, chilli zing of Mexico, Zahtar Starter has got fancy, with toasted sesame seeds, sumac berries and thyme.

Red sumac berries are that gorgeous shade of red that's the colour of rubies, old pubs and velvet. The fresh red berries have a fine coating of malic acid, the stuff that gives apples their tang, and hence they have a sharp lemony hit to them. White sumac berries, in contrast, are deeply poisonous and not to be eaten. Red sumac berries mixed with toasted sesame seeds and dried thyme is a classic Middle Eastern mixture, used in much the same way as the French classic herbes de Provence – that is they add a pinch in just about everything. You can taste why. It is now possible to buy ready-mixed zahtar, as blended by Seasoned Pioneers.

When buying avocados for Zahtar Starter, get nice ripe, squashy ones. The best way to eat avocados is when they're **really ripe, creamy and full of flavour.**

It's also the best kind for using on your face. Yep, just whack the raw, squashed avocado flesh onto your forehead to help eradicate any fine lines. They stimulate the DNA in your skin cells to manufacture collagen, saving you a lot of time, effort, money and potential face-ache from botox. Oh, and you can use the empty avocado skins to moisturize your knees and elbows. Nice.

Avocado pears will nourish your insides, too. They're full of vitamins A, C and E, the ones that help your body fight free radicals – and I don't mean independent thinkers. Avocados have plenty of potassium in them too, a major mineral for helping your brain deal with stress and too much burning the candle at both ends. Hmm, think I'll go and eat this right now.

ZAHTAR STARTER

Juice of ¼ a lemon

2 tablespoons olive oil

1 teaspoon toasted sesame seeds

¼ teaspoon ground red sumac berries

¼ teaspoon dried thyme

1 garlic clove, crushed

Black pepper to taste

1 ripe avocado

1–2 tablespoons dark tahini

25g goat's feta cheese, well crumbled

In a cup, thoroughly mix the lemon juice, oil, sesame seeds, sumac berries, thyme, garlic and pepper with a fork. Put it to one side for at least 10 minutes so everything can mingle.

Cut your avocado with a sharp knife from top to bottom, cutting right through to the stone. Twist the two halves apart and remove the stone. Carefully slice the flesh in parallel lines through to the skin, but avoid cutting the skin if possible. Now slice in the same way but at right angles, to form a criss-cross of squares.

Turn the avocado halves inside out so that they look a little bit like green hedgehogs (well they do if your kitchen lighting is quite dim). With your fingers, tear the fleshy cubes from the skin into a bowl, removing any dodgy black bits. Lick your fingers, then give them a good soapy wash. Give the lemony oil a quick stir with a fork, then pour the mixture into the avocado bowl. Add the tahini and cheese and blend everything together with a fork. Serve immediately with pitta breads, Quinoa Grissini (see page 254) and a chunky Greek salad.

PS If you want, get retro by growing your avocado stone into a 1970s-style houseplant. Simply poke three toothpicks into its sides around the middle, then dangle it, point side up, over a pot of water, with its bottom submerged. Thassit.

CHERRY CHOCOLATE SPREAD

I hear sniggering at the back … But I promise you that despite being tofu-based, this chocolate spread is gloriously decadent and rich. And unlike most chocolate spreads, it's guaranteed to leave you feeling happy instead of slightly queasy. Rest assured, it tastes divine, especially when served with hot organic croissants, transforming them into pain au chocolats.

Don't be tempted to use mass-produced tofu, as this stuff gives beautiful artisan-made tofu a bad name. When I was in Tokyo, I used to shop at my local tofu shop. There's a hand-made-tofu shop on every high street, just like the bakery shop that used to sit on every British street. Each Japanese tofu shop has a myriad of different kinds of tofu, including gooey and strong-tasting natto, and the lightest, creamiest silken tofus. My local one had a musty wooden interior and the tofu-maker wore traditional dark blue Japanese clothing. The whole air of this place was of tradition and skill.

It's not just what you put in that counts with tofu. It's how it's made. All organic tofu is GM-free by definition, but Fresh & Wild has the widest range of hand-made, fine quality tofus I know of in the UK. Paul's is my personal favourite from their selection. Proper tofu-making is a slow craft, just like cheese-making. It takes time for the nigari mineral to curdle the soy milk, just as it takes time for the rennet to curdle the cow's milk.

Green & Black's make the dark chocolate with whole cherries that I've used for this spread. You can try making it with other dark or milk chocolate from Fresh & Wild, as they all have a high enough cocoa content to melt and flavour this recipe, so experiment. You know it makes sense.

Chocolate-tasting is an art, just like wine-tasting. But it's more fun.

Chocolate is generally judged on a few set criteria, which are: appearance, aroma, flavour, texture and the length of the melt. Last year, I suffered for you, dear reader, by tasting about 20 different kinds of organic chocolate in one sitting – which I really don't recommend.

It was all in the name of research, the aim of which was to find the greatest organic chocolates and let y'all know. It was properly organized with a panel of tasters, lots of organic white bread to cleanse palates between blocks and a top chocolate taster to guide us through the work at hand. It was torment, but we did sample some pretty awesome chocolate, alongside a few poor offerings. Try brands like Rococo, Chocaid, Montezuma's and Rapunzel for more great-tasting fairly traded chocolates.

Well-farmed organic ingredients definitely do taste better, as they've been grown in richer soil for healthier plants that are able to imbue their produce with more phyto-chemicals and hence more flavour. But, like the tofu, it's what you do with these great-tasting ingredients that counts. Suck it and see seems to be the rule of thumb with organic chocolate, so get adventurous with the lovely chocolates on offer at

Fresh & Wild. But if you're going for the full taste-challenge monty, remember to chew and spit if you want to avoid overloading.

Whichever kind of chocolate you go for in this recipe, if you want a **crunchier texture**, try whizzing the chocolate in a **food processor** instead of melting it.

You'll end up with a crunchy, peanut butter texture that's just as lovely as the regular, meltingly smooth consistency. White chocolate won't melt properly, as the cocoa solids are too low to combine well with the rest of the spread, but if you whizz it, you can use it to make a crunchy, peanut-butter-textured white chocolate spread. Lovely.

CHERRY CHOCOLATE SPREAD

TO MAKE A BOWL OF CHERRY CHOCOLATE SPREAD:

100g Green & Black's dark chocolate with whole cherries
350g firm, hand-made tofu
100g corn and barley malt syrup
50g sesame halva (and eat the rest)

Break the chocolate into pieces and put it into a heatproof bowl. Put the bowl over a saucepan of gently simmering water and melt the chocolate, stirring it with a metal spoon. Put all the other ingredients into a food processor and whizz to your heart's content.

Pour and scrape the melted chocolate into the creamy tofu mixture and zap briefly again to mix everything up. Pop the spread in the fridge and it'll be ready in 20 minutes.

FRESH CRAB PÂTÉ

This is another recipe for which your local Fresh & Wild fish counter is invaluable. Ask the resident fishmonger to give you two empty crab shells, saved from the fresh crab meat on display. You can use them to hold the pâté while it's baking, making the finished dish look really evocative of the seashore.

On the down side, this pâté is high in cholesterol, so don't eat it if your doctor's mentioned the phrase 'low cholesterol diet' in your ear. Crab meat is high in cholesterol, as are butter and cream. To be precise, there's roughly 1 milligram of cholesterol to every gram of crab. And, in this recipe, you also need to add cholesterol-rich butter and cream.

On the good side, there's a consensus that an average person, whoever that may be, needs to limit their cholesterol to 300mg per day – which means that you could happily eat a portion of this pâté and still have plenty of leeway for another portion, well as long as you don't spend the rest of the day eating cholesterol-rich foods.

However, this is decent food that tastes so rich you'll eat a few mouthfuls and be happy. You won't want to yam it all up and ask for seconds. No. Your brain will respond by telling your body it's satisfied.

Crab meat is full of high-quality protein, plus vitamin B_{12}, and is mineral rich, as you might expect from an animal that has spent its life in the mineral-rich sea. There's lots of zinc, phosphorus, calcium and iron, so, amongst other things, it's great for making sperm (if you're a man) and keeping your nails nice, whichever gender you might be.

This pâté can be eaten hot or cold and goes well with Caraway Potato Bagels (page 257), light leafy salads (pages 211 and 219) and white wine.

FRESH CRAB PÂTÉ

1 tablespoon lightly salted butter

1 teaspoon plain flour

A pinch of mace

75ml single cream

1 teaspoon spiced honey mustard

2 slices good wholemeal bread

200g fresh white crab meat

A handful of tarragon, finely chopped

2 large clean crab shells

Put the oven on to 200°C/400°F/Gas Mark 6. Melt the butter in a medium saucepan, over a medium heat, then stir in the flour and mace with a wooden spoon. When it's combined, stir the cream in little by little. Slowly bring the cream to the boil so that it thickens. Stir in the mustard and simmer for a few minutes.

Whizz the bread in a food processor to make breadcrumbs. Put the crumbs into a big bowl with the crabmeat and tarragon, then mix well. Pour the cream sauce in and stir until everything's combined. Spoon the pâté into the empty crab shells, balance them open-side up on a baking tray and whack 'em into the oven. They'll be ready in about 20 minutes.

BABA GANOUSH

If you like hummus and taramasalata, you'll love this. A traditional starter served throughout the Middle East, baba ganoush is a rich dip often eaten with pitta or flat breads, olives and feta. Aubergine can be a bit bitter for some, but is much sweeter when baked for baba ganoush. The dense starches in the vegetable caramelize and sweeten with heat, producing a slightly sticky flavour and a smooth, creamy texture. If you're not keen on tahini, try using Greek yogurt instead for a baba ganoush/tzatziki cross.

Try to use male aubergines instead of female ones if you can. I'm completely serious. Aubergines, like a good few plants, grow as single gender plants. They're grown separately so that the genders don't mix uncontrollably, as they would if grown together.

The fruits of boy aubergine plants are those aubergines with a little dimply point at the non-stem end of the vegetable. You're sure to have seen them and thought that the little pointy bit is cute. Girl aubergines are the ones that are much more seedy inside, with a really rounded end and no sign of a pointy bit.

Simply examine the aubergine before you buy them and get the boy ones if you can, as they're nicer. That said, during some months, only girls are available, so try it with them too.

BABA GANOUSH

TO MAKE ENOUGH FOR TWO PEOPLE'S LUNCHES:

1 medium aubergine
Juice of a freshly squeezed lemon
3 heaped tablespoons tahini
2 garlic cloves, crushed
1 teaspoon good sea salt
1 tablespoon cold-pressed olive oil
A handful of fresh parsley

Heat the oven to 200°C/400°F/Gas Mark 6. Put the aubergine directly on the rack in the middle of the oven and every 10 minutes, open the oven and turn the aubergine quickly so you don't lose too much heat. Keep doing this until the aubergine is very soft. Being careful not to burn your fingers, peel the skin and pull off the stem.

Put the aubergine flesh into a bowl and mash it with a fork. Stir in half the lemon juice and then gradually add all the tahini, mashing all the time. In a cup, grind the garlic with the salt using a teaspoon. It will make a crunchy paste. Add the olive oil to the garlic and mix well. Scoop the contents of the cup into the aubergine mixture, add the parsley and mash together. Finally, add the rest of the lemon juice, little by little, to taste.

PUKKA **DUKKAH** SPREAD

At the risk of sounding like a certain popular 'geezer' chef, Pukka Dukkah Spread is sure to spice up your lunch. It's shockingly simple to make and tastes the bomb. Based around the classic Egyptian spice mix, called dukkah of course, this nutty, fragrant sandwich spread is perfect for a summer picnic or a toasted bruschetta lunch in winter.

Dukkah is a sprinkle more than a spice blend, as it's not just powder. It includes little sesame seeds, chopped hazelnuts and dried thyme leaves, as well as finely ground coriander seeds, white cumin, black pepper and salt. It's often to be found on the table in Cairo restaurants, alongside a bowl of olive oil and a stack of flat breads ready for dunking. Here it's mixed up with lentils to create a filling spread fit for any time of the day.

This recipe shows how we naturally pair up vegetarian ingredients that complement each other in terms of their protein balance. The general rule of thumb when balancing amino acids in a vegetarian meal is to have two foods from each of the three protein-rich food groups – these are pulses, grains and seeds. So baked beans on toast will give you a balance of amino acids, as the beans are a pulse and the toast is a grain. And rice and peas does the job right too, as does pukka dukkah spread with Phat Green Flat Bread (see page 242).

Lentils feature in numerous cuisines, from gourmet French Puy lentil stews to richly-spiced Indian dhals. However, despite their widespread popularity since ancient times, there's no denying they can give you wind if eaten on their own.

This recipe should nip any such problem in the bud, as the coriander, cumin, bay leaves and garlic generally counteract those uncomfortable feelings. This is just one more reason why various cuisines use nature's herby and spicy helpers for health as well as taste. So always add one of these herbs or spices when cooking with lentils, or any of the other flatulence-busters, including kombu and ajowan seeds.

PUKKA **DUKKAH** SPREAD

FOR 4 HUNGRY PEOPLE:

250g red split lentils
2 bay leaves
500g Joubere (or 500ml homemade) chicken stock, homemade or Joubere's
2 tablespoons olive oil
1 medium onion, peeled and finely diced
4 medium garlic cloves, crushed
1 medium tomato, finely chopped
1 red chilli, deseeded, membranes removed and finely chopped
4 teaspoons dukkah spice mix
A handful of flat-leaf parsley

Simmer the lentils and bay leaves in the stock over a medium heat. Keep the lid on the saucepan so you don't lose too much steam and let the lentils simmer for about 25 minutes, or until tender. The stock should all vanish into the lentils. When they're done, take the pan off the heat and remove the bay leaves using a fork so that you don't burn yourself.

In a big frying pan, heat the oil over a medium heat. Add the onion and garlic and fry, stirring with a wooden spoon, for about 4 minutes. Add the tomato and chilli and keep cooking for another few minutes. Add the dukkah and fry for another minute or so. Be careful not to burn the ingredients. It's better to undercook than overcook this part of the dish, as burnt garlic and spices taste acrid.

Turn down the heat to low. Add the cooked lentils and the parsley and mix together well, over the heat, using a wooden spoon. Turn the heat off, then spoon the spread into a ceramic bowl and leave it to cool. Serve with salad greens, cucumber, olives and sprouted seeds, plus a wedge of lemon on the side.

UMEBOSHI SQUASHY SPREAD

If you've never taken the plunge, treat yourself to a jar of Japan's finest umeboshi (pronounced *oo-meh-bo-shee*) plum paste, or the whole plums themselves. You will not be disappointed. They're not the cheapest plums on the planet, but they are definitely one of the most delicious, strongly flavoured and versatile.

A beautiful deep-pink colour, umeboshi plum paste is very salty yet still kinda sweet and very tart. In fact, it's a one-of-a-kind taste sensation. As such, a little goes a long way.

It's also **incredibly good for you**, particularly your **stomach, liver and kidneys**, which makes it all the easier to feel happy when snacking on this salty spread.

UMEBOSHI SQUASHY SPREAD

FOR SPREADING ON BREAD FOR 2:

150g tofu
3 tablespoons live yogurt
1–2 teaspoons umeboshi plum paste
1–2 teaspoons toasted sesame oil
2 teaspoons green nori flakes

Mash the tofu in a shallow bowl with a fork. Stir the yogurt in its tub to mix in any liquid that's separated out, then add 3 tablespoons to the tofu. Add a teaspoon of umeboshi paste, a teaspoon of sesame oil and all the nori flakes. Stir and mash everything together with the fork. Have a taste and add more umeboshi and sesame if you think it needs more. Mash and stir again, then serve with Dr Karg's crispbreads or warm Caribe Chilli Tortillas (see page 252).

This spread is also lovely with thin slices of fresh cucumber, chopped pak choi or grated celeriac. Or, for another Japanese note, try adding a slice of takuan, a traditional kind of pickled daikon that's a bit like a gherkin.

YEASTY **BUTTER BEAN** SPREAD

The nutritional yeast flakes featured in this recipe will not make your bread rise. They look a bit like dried fish food and smell about as appetizing when they're in the tub. But mix nutritional yeast flakes with some moist ingredients and they spring into life, adding a rich and sort of cheesy flavour to just about anything savoury.

They're made by growing a snappily named strain of yeast (Saccharomyces cerevisiae) on mineral-enriched molasses, then drying and flaking the yeast. It's exactly the same kind of yeast that makes up brewer's yeast, the only difference being the flavour. Brewer's yeast is a by-product of the beer industry, so it tastes of bitter hops, whereas nutritional yeast flakes have a sweeter and generally tastier taste.

Most people who have an excess of candida in their bodies find that nutritional yeast flakes do not cause any adverse reactions. If you are concerned about this, check your personal tolerance levels with a qualified medical nutritionist but, generally, most people can eat nutritional yeast flakes with no problem because it's a completely different kind of yeast from the stuff that causes candida.

Yeast flakes are pretty essential eating for vegetarians and particularly vegans and will also undoubtedly improve the nutritional profile of just about any other kind of diet, as they're rammed full of B vitamins. The whole of the B vitamin spectrum can be found here, except for B_{12}, and also 14 different minerals and 16 out of the 20 amino acids. Basically, these guys are great and also taste lovely. And remember – B vitamins are the ones that help you deal with life's little challenges without letting them get you down.

YEASTY **BUTTER BEAN** SPREAD

200g dried butter beans, soaked overnight or a tin of butter beans

2 tablespoons olive oil

1 small onion, peeled and finely chopped

2 garlic cloves, peeled and crushed

1 stick of celery, de-stringed and finely chopped

1 tablespoon brown rice vinegar

2 tablespoons nutritional yeast flakes

If you're using dried butter beans, simmer the pre-soaked beans in 500ml of water for an hour, in a medium-sized saucepan, covered with a lid. If you're using canned beans, open the tin and drain away the liquid. Either way, start the rest of this recipe when you've got a bunch of cooked beans ready in a bowl.

Heat the oil in a medium frying pan, over a medium heat. Once it's hot, add the onions and fry for a couple of minutes, stirring with a wooden spoon. Add the garlic and celery and keep frying for a few more minutes until everything is translucent and smells cooked. Before the onions go brown, add the contents of the pan to the beans, scraping the tasty oil out of the pan and into the bowl with your trusty wooden spoon. Throw in the vinegar and the yeast flakes and mash everything together with a fork.

Once the spread has cooled down, spread it on warm Caribe Chilli Tortillas (see page 252), top with a raw root salad and roll up to give a delicious wrap.

KOOKY **ADUKI**

Aduki are brilliant because not only do they come in one of my favourite colours, they also don't need soaking before you use them. You're free to knock up this pâté on a whim, as it takes only an hour between the idea coming into your head and hot kooky aduki on toast. And if you make up a big batch, it freezes no problem.

Why kooky? Because it's sweet. In Asian cuisine, aduki beans are often made into sweet pastes for filling cakes.

They're **good in savoury dishes** too, but this recipe is their chance to **get sweet** with you.

However, if you really fancy trying a savoury version, simply leave out the malt syrup and add a pinch of salt and pepper instead.

KOOKY **ADUKI**

TO MAKE LOADS OF PÂTÉ:

300g aduki beans
3 tablespoons sunflower oil
1 tablespoon toasted sesame oil
1 tablespoon ground cinnamon
50g ground almonds
2 tablespoons brown rice vinegar
4 tablespoons brown rice malt syrup

Simmer the beans in 1 litre of water, in a large covered saucepan, for an hour. Heat the oils in a big frying pan and tip in the cinnamon and ground almonds when it's hot. Stir with a wooden spoon, adding the vinegar after a minute. While it's sizzling, mix in the syrup and add a little bit of water so that it's not too sticky. Be careful the liquid doesn't spit at you.

Drain the unwanted bean water away, then tip the adukis into the frying pan. Turn off the heat and mix everything with a wooden spoon. Zap everything in a food processor, or thoroughly mash the mixture with a fork. Eat hot if you're impatient, or chilled for a firmer texture.

KIDS' STUFF

Children on the Makaibari tea estate, Darjeeling, India

How do you get children to eat real food?

Some parents are blessed with little angels that can't get enough of fresh fruit and veg, whole grain breads, fruit smoothies and tofu stir-fries, but sadly they seem to be in the minority. Often it's tough getting kids to eat their food up – battle commences, bargains are struck, portions are hidden under forks and tantrums occur.

So just how do you get your kids to eat well?

The first step is identifying the good ingredients that they do like. If your kid says they don't like vegetables, but they'll always reach for the peas when push comes to shove, make them more pea-type things – whether it's mange-tout, French beans, broad beans or edamame, give them anything that resembles a pea. If they prefer cucumbers, try serving marrow and courgettes, or other watery vegetables like pak choi, celery or mild lettuces.

Don't forget that kids need their five portions of fruit and veg every day just as much as you do. A kid's portion is generally classified as the amount they can hold in their hand. They need this much fresh produce to keep their immunity up and maintain their health and energy for all that learning, playing and growing.

There are so many good organic convenience foods out there that buying junk food for your children doesn't make any sense. So simply don't keep dodgy stuff in the house. If it's convenience you're after, without the rubbish ingredients, go for things like Clearspring's amazing fruit purées, seaweed and sesame crisps, oblongs of decent organic cheeses and freshly-made fruit and vegetable juices. Also, keep your fruit bowls at kid-friendly heights and show them where the ready-scrubbed finger veg live in the fridge, like new-season carrots, de-stringed celery sticks, topped and tailed French beans and trimmed spring onions.

However, the most important thing to bear in mind is the mantra for getting kids keen on good food: theatre, fantasy and disguise.

T H E A T R E

Every proper sit-down meal is an opportunity for theatre. I'm not talking about your little one playing a prima donna about having to eat carrots. No – I'm talking about setting the scene for a fun time. In the same way that grown-ups enjoy their food more when they get to wear a nice outfit, drink some wine and eat by candlelight, kids invariably eat more grub with less fuss when you treat them to an enjoyable setting. And if they sit down to eat, there's much less chance of them choking on bits of food than if they're running around.

Talking of safety, you should help your kids cut up their food into small enough pieces, or do it for them if they've not yet got the coordination skills to handle a fork and knife. Always sit with your kids whilst they're eating to make sure they're eating safely and encourage them to eat by having a little portion yourself. It's like the sleeping principle – if you lie down with little ones for an afternoon nap, they're much more likely to fall asleep. And if you eat a bit of food when they do, they're much more likely to eat up.

Tara Meehan used to work at Fresh & Wild before her growing family lured her away from the workplace to become a full-time mum. As such, Tara's got a great understanding of good food and raising kids, and is an expert at providing theatrical eating experiences for her two young children, Olivia and Eve.

They have themed nights, such as Chinese Night or Italian Night. When Tara cooks a Chinese meal for the girls, they turn up to dinner in their silky Chinese pyjamas with rookie chopsticks at the ready. Rookie chop-sticks are available in the shops and are basically trainer chopsticks that are joined at one end to make them easy to use. The food is served in lit-tle rice bowls, facilitating play for the girls. Chinese background music plays on the CD player and the kids have little egg cups filled with weak miso soup masquerading as Chinese tea.

On Italian Night, the kids get to make loads of tomato sauce mess as they grapple with spaghetti bolognaise. The scene is set with candlelight and Vivaldi, the girls wearing pretty long nighties that are make-believe princess dresses. The spaghetti is eaten with forks and spoons, with the kids twirling the pasta as best they can. It's served with tricolore salad on the side – slices of mozzarella, tomato and avocado with fresh basil leaves, drizzled with olive oil – and special small sherry glasses filled with grape juice instead of wine. Of course, it goes without saying that you need to be at the table all the time children are eating by candlelight to make sure there are no accidents.

There's nothing that says you can't be stretched by the idea of theatrical meals. Explore a cuisine you're not familiar with, such as Mongolian or Azerbaijani, and search out some appropriate music, costumes and facts from that culture. That way you get to learn whilst encouraging your children to eat, and you all get to enjoy a taste of another culture.

There's a lot to be said for creative presentation and the fun of theatre. Instead of serving fruit compote with yogurt on the side, layer the compote and yogurt in tall glasses and serve with a long spoon. Knickerbocker glo-ries are lots more fun!

FANTASY

Every child has a powerful imagination that's just waiting to be harnessed, and a magical way to get them interested in food is to show them how it's made. You can start by growing things with them. Herbs are a good starting point, either in the garden or in a window box. Tomato plants, peppers and chillies grow well in a sunny window and strawberries are good in pots, too. Beans grow nice and quickly so are fun for kids to grow, and potatoes offer the excitement of discovery as they dig them up.

You can also play with presentation by forming foods into fun shapes. Homemade fish cakes can be made into fish shapes and homemade chicken patties turned into chicken shapes before you can say 'chicken nuggets'. Make faces with food, as kids love smiley faces more than anything: try pastry faces baked into pies, salads with tomato eyes and radish noses, sandwiches with pâté cheeks and red pepper smiles, breakfast porridge with barley malt syrup mouths and sultana eyes ... The possibilities are limited only by your sense of humour and what's available in your fridge.

When a child's played a part in making something, they invariably want to play a part in eating it. When you're cooking, always get your child involved in the safe and easy bits, whatever their age. A baby can press the zap button on a food processor. A toddler can press a carrot into a juicer with your help, but for goodness sake, watch those fingers and use the proper plunger tool.

And you'll find that almost every child can lick the bowl if you've been baking! Getting your little ones to shake the salad dressing in a jar (with a tight lid screwed on) can mean the difference between their salad being eaten or left to one side. Never underestimate how much more exciting food can be if they've helped prepare it, but never take risks with their dexterity or judgement skills – kids haven't yet developed enough of either of these to be able to deal safely with sharp objects, heat or spatial distances. So please encourage them to get involved in the kitchen, but only when you can give them your very best attention.

Most importantly, if you want your child to eat something decent, ask them what they want to eat out of your fridge and cupboard selection. If they're part of the decision process when choosing their lunch, they're much more likely to eat it.

When you use fantasy, you're engaging your child in the land of make believe. My mum used to play aeroplanes with my sisters and me. A piece of the food that I'd been avoiding was put onto the fork and flown into my mouth by my mum, complete with whizzing noises. Tara finds that word games work well with Olivia and Eve. She'll tell a story that includes the names of the food on their plates – something like 'Olivia and Eve were walking down the road when they saw a man holding some CARROTS!' At this point, they both eat carrots like there's no tomorrow.

D I S G U I S E

Fooling your kids is not a last resort. It's a fact of life. Lots of children don't like tomatoes but love tomato ketchup. Get around this problem by purée-ing fresh tomatoes, or making fresh tomato-based sauces that are strained to remove any tell-tale seeds. If your kids don't like greens such as spinach, kale or chard, Tara suggests steaming the greens, then whizzing them in a food processor with crème fraîche or yogurt to make a sauce.

Don't tell them the origins of things you think they might be squeamish about. Like adults, most kids aren't keen to try sea vegetables if they know they're seaweed. But it's a rare child that doesn't love chewing sheets of toasted nori, especially if they've had a hand in toasting them (with a pair of tongs and an adult doing the main flame-grilling bit).

Marinating poultry, meat, fish and soy products like tofu and tempeh doesn't exactly disguise them, but it's another opportunity to get your child involved with the dinner-making process and transforming the central ingredients.

From **squeezing lemon** juice to mixing shoyu marinades and **crushing garlic**, kids can **get involved** with flavours, adjusting them to their liking.

Just make sure they watch out for any stray lemon juice so they don't squirt their eyes and get any little fingers out of the way if using a garlic press to crush cloves of garlic.

Also, sauce bottles with nozzle attachments make meal times a lot more fun. Fill your sauce bottle with homemade or good quality sauces, then let the kids squeeze out their names on toast, make a flower drawing for mashed root vegetables, or a funny face for their hemp ice cream.

And try other interactive disguises, like leaving bowls of sprinkles on the table at dinner and lunch times for them to dip into. Furikake is a good ready-made sesame sprinkle, plus there are ready-toasted green nori flakes, and try saucers of herbs and pepper, or little bowls of spirulina or KidGreenz.

Children love playing with the **vitamin supplement Emergen-C**, which is like fizzy sugar.

Go easy with it, but a little bit every now and then is a fun way for them to take a vitamin C supplement. Make sure you just give them enough to mix a child-sized drink, and not the whole packet, 'cause they might just have the lot if you let them – especially as it comes in loads of different flavours.

Most children love juices, both fruit and vegetable, especially when they've had a hand in making them. Dilute juices with cucumber juice and water when serving them to kids, as they're too sweet and strongly flavoured for their palates if served straight. And fruit smoothies with banana and yogurt generally go down a treat, whether made with any kind of ambient yogurt or with frozen yogurt like Fresh & Wild's juice bars.

Of course, there comes a time when theatre, fantasy and disguises come to an end and information needs to be forthcoming. You can start building awareness about food, taste and health at a young age. If your children have a solid background experience of food times as good times, it's simpler to add an understanding of the building blocks of an enjoyable, good and healthy diet. Start building this food awareness while you're still playing with theatre, fantasy and disguise and the transition to regular good food should be smooth and trouble-free.

Generally speaking, don't indulge in 'dumbing down' your kids' dinners. Serve small portions of your own dinner, but maybe with less hot spices depending on their preferences. Start your kids with decent and complex flavours right from the beginning of their lives by using dried mango as a teething soother. As they grow, add a few items that are specifically made for your children as treats or medicines, like the recipe ideas featured in this chapter.

VEGETABLE **JELLY**

If your kids are funny about eating their veg, make it more fun by adding it to savoury jellies, or vegetable aspics, as some people prefer calling them. This recipe is a great combination of theatre, fantasy and disguise. You can go on a Japanese journey about the agar-agar flakes used to make it, or get fantastic with tales of extra-terrestrial jelly monsters in pea-green space ships. All the potentially troublesome vegetables are cunningly disguised, allowing your little ones to enjoy the make-believe whilst unwittingly eating up their greens.

That said, there's nothing more fun for little fingers than podding peas. If they're in season, install your children in the kitchen for podding duties. And if they're not in season, rest assured that organic frozen peas are just as nutritious as the fresh version.

Of course, this is basically a recipe for little round vegetable terrines, a very respectably adult dish. Well that's a contradiction in terms actually, as the word terrine refers to the long earthenware troughs it's usually made in. Oh well, not this one – unless you've got some, in which case, go ahead.

You could try it with steamed organic gourmet mushrooms layered in an agar-agar jelly instead, either served up for your kids or saved for the next time your pals are coming round. Alternatively, try it with grilled aubergine slices, steamed asparagus spears and tender, shredded chicken breasts.

This humble vegetable jelly recipe is a small part of my cunning plan to re-kindle the art of jelly making, whether savoury or sweet. Victorian jelly-makers went completely over the top when it came to both ice cream and jelly making. They coloured both of these foods with bright natural vegetable dyes, then created garish food sculptures out of them of almost Baroque proportions and complexities. You sometimes see their copper moulds on sale in antique shops, frilly to the max and sadly with a price tag to match. But there's no need to follow their example – us contemporary cooks can have fun with jelly in a modern style, getting fresh with fresh ingredients and moulding them into just about any shape we please, thank you very much.

This dish is a good starter jelly and hopefully will encourage you to create more and more outlandish jelly dishes for your kids amusement and also your own. This recipe's not fancy at all, and gives you something useful to do with those little earthenware dip dishes and glass or ceramic ramekins that are almost definitely littering up the back of your cupboard. You could also use your kids' Play-dough moulds, carefully scrubbed of any Play-dough remnants, of course.

VEGETABLE **JELLY**

FOR 2 SIDE PORTIONS OF VEGETABLE JELLY:

50g fresh shelled peas, steamed, or 50g frozen peas, defrosted
50g diced carrots, steamed
150ml of the water from the steamed veg
2 teaspoons agar-agar flakes

Put the veg into a blender and zap until they're indistinguishable. Find two jelly moulds that are about 100ml in capacity and fill them with the veg. These could be proper little old-fashioned jelly moulds, or any other little receptacles that'll work.

Let the water from the vegetables cool in a pan until lukewarm, then sprinkle the agar-agar onto the water. Put the pan onto a low heat and wait for the water to simmer. When it starts simmering, stir the agar-agar now and then. After a few minutes, take the pan off the heat.

Pour the jelly mix over the steamed vegetables and leave to cool on a work surface. When the moulds are at room temperature, put them carefully in the fridge. They should be firmly set after 2–3 hours. When they're set, gently coax them out by pulling the edges slowly away from the mould. Then turn the mould upside down over a plate and shake them to slide the jellies out.

STICKY CHESTNUTS

Laziness isn't a great thing, but I'm delighted that you can now buy ready-cooked and peeled chestnuts at Fresh & Wild. The dried ones taste almost as lovely, but they take forever to cook and peel one by one. When prepared with ready-to-go chestnuts, this recipe is made in a flash, keeping your little ones happy.

Kids love eating with their fingers, whatever their age. Make sure their little hands are clean and give them napkins with the bowl of chestnuts – otherwise you stand no chance of keeping your furniture non-sticky. If you've got fabric napkins, they're a good way of reducing waste paper and make sense when dealing with the messy food habits of children.

STICKY CHESTNUTS

1 teaspoon cold-pressed olive oil

1 teaspoon toasted sesame oil

1 teaspoon of Seasoned Pioneers la kama spice blend

1 packet ready-cooked and peeled Sierra Rica chestnuts

A pinch of proper sea salt

¼ a small lime

Heat the oils over a medium–low heat in a small frying pan. Once hot, quickly fry the spices for a few seconds, being very careful not to burn them. Add the chestnuts and salt and stir to coat them in spices. Raise the heat a little and squeeze the lime juice into the pan. As soon as the liquid hits the pan, quickly coat the chestnuts so they can go slightly sticky with caramelized lime juice. When the liquid has totally evaporated, take the chestnuts off the heat and serve.

PUNKY P E O P L E

These punky people are made from alfalfa and are definitely members of the food fantasy club. They won't fill your kids up, but the process of seeing the wiggly alfalfa hair grow will help them connect more with their salad.

TO MAKE 2 PUNKY PEOPLE:

Cotton wool
2 clean eggshells, collected after a boiled egg breakfast and washed
1 teaspoon alfalfa seeds

First get your child to draw a funny face onto the eggshells. Now get your child to stuff each one with some cotton wool. You now need to moisten the fibre and sprinkle a few alfalfa seeds on top. As long as they remember (with your help) to keep the cotton wool moist, within a week their egg-pal will have grown green hair, ready to be snipped off with scissors for sandwiches.

MOCHI

You won't believe how good these little beauties are. They're one of my favourite foods of all time, so don't let the kids hog them all. Made from brown rice, these iron-age Japanese cakes are a challenge to the rules of evolution. Just how did the first person discover that pounding a particular kind of rice, then soaking and steaming it, could form the basis of a delectable snack? Answers on a postcard, please.

In theory you can make mochi cakes at home, and most Japanese people do when it comes to special holidays like New Year's Eve. However, it's quite a palaver. Life's made easy for us, as Clearspring make two excellent varieties of ready-pounded mochi. There's plain mochi and mochi with added mugwort. I recommend starting your kids on the plain ones, as the mugwort ones are more strongly flavoured. If you're making these for adults, add some grated ginger root, tekka and sushi pickles on the side.

Do your kids a favour and give this a try.

MOCHI

SERVES 2–4 CHILDREN, DEPENDING ON THEIR SIZES:

1 tablespoon toasted sesame oil
1 tablespoon sunflower frying oil
2 plain mochi cakes
¼ teaspoon umeboshi plum paste
A few drops of tamari
2 sheets nori seaweed

Heat the oils, over a low heat, in a frying pan that has a lid. Add both of the mochi cakes, put the lid on the pan and continue to cook over a low heat for a few minutes, when the bottoms should start to go crispy. Make sure you don't over-cook them, as they'll go very chewy instead of a light fudge texture.

Meanwhile, mix the umeboshi and tamari in a saucer. Flip the mochi cakes with a spatula and replace the lid. Toast the nori sheets, holding them, one at a time, over a gas flame or electric hob for a few seconds. Be careful not to burn your fingers – small kids should never ever do this bit for obvious safety reasons, and adults need to use tongs when showing kids nori-toasting.

The nori will go a bit crispy and change colour to a slightly metallic-looking bright green. Be careful not to let the nori burn, and make sure your kids watch this magical transformation happen. Spread the paste you have made in equal amounts onto the nori sheets.

The mochi cakes will probably be done now, so get them out of the pan and roll them in the nori. Leave them to cool slightly, which will also allow the nori time to seal around them. If serving four little people, cut these two servings in half. Serve with mild Japanese tea or freshly pressed apple juice.

TAMARI NUTS AND SEEDS

This is an oldie but a goodie. Try the method used in this recipe for jazzing up any other kind of seeds or nuts, from sesame to Brazils, and kiss goodbye the dry-roasted peanuts of yesteryear.

Walnuts have lots of heart-healthy potassium and iron in them, plus the same amount of protein weight for weight as eggs. And both the walnuts and the seeds are full of the top quality omega oils that will keep your little ones flexible and on the go. Sunflower seeds are also full of zinc, so they're good for preventing colds.

Like all nuts and seeds, they provide loads of the energy your children need to keep them alert, as well as being a delicious finger food to entertain their taste buds. But please don't leave kids on their own when they're eating small things like seeds and nuts, just in case. It also goes without saying that you shouldn't serve them up to little ones with allergies, so if you're entertaining your child's friends, call a parent before they arrive to double check if they have any allergies.

Don't let the kids hog these little diamonds. They're good with martinis for the grown-ups, too. In fact, they're pretty good sprinkled on most savoury things, from soups and salads to brown rice and stir-fries. Easy.

TAMARI NUTS AND SEEDS

FOR A BOWL OF TAMARI NUTS AND SEEDS:

125g walnut pieces

125g sunflower seeds

1 tablespoon sesame seeds

1 tablespoon tamari, plus a bit more if you want

1 tablespoon mirin

1 tablespoon toasted nori flakes

Heat a heavy frying pan over a medium heat and then add the nuts and seeds to the dry pan. Move them about with a wooden spoon and add the tamari and mirin as soon as you can smell the nuts and seeds begin to toast.

Keep turning them in the sauce, coating them in brown stickiness as the excess liquid evaporates. Add a bit more tamari if your child likes their nuts and seeds rich and salty. Take the pan off the heat as soon as all the liquid has gone, then toss in the nori flakes and turn the nuts and seeds to coat them. Leave to cool in a bowl, then serve with a glass of water.

R O A S T E D **CHIPS**

Roasting vegetables makes them softer and more kid-friendly, but it also concentrates their flavours and makes them sweeter whilst still keeping lots of their goodness. And once they've cooled down, they make great food to just grab and chew.

Please bin any non-organic oven chips you might have hanging around your freezer. They've got loads of hydrogenated and/or saturated fats in them, which you really don't want to be feeding your lovely kids.

Instead, go for these easy-to-make vegetable chips. Simply chop any organic root vegetables into fat chips, roll them in enough olive oil to cover each chip, then lay them on a baking sheet. Bake in an oven set to 200°C/400°F/Gas Mark 6 for about 25 minutes or longer, depending on the hardness of the vegetable and the thickness of the cut. You'll know they're ready when the kitchen smells delicious and the chips are soft inside when they're broken (or eaten by you – just to test them of course).

ROASTED PUMPKIN SEEDS

When you make a meal using pumpkin or squash, get your kids to scrape out the seeds and cook them. Cut the pumpkin or squash in half, then the kids can use metal spoons and their fingers to pull out the seeds and all their fibres. They'll now need to wash them so put the seeds and fibres into a big bowl and add some warm water so their hands won't get cold.

They'll need two bowls, one on either side of the seeds. The first is for the stringy pulp that binds the seeds to the pumpkin, the other is for the cleaned seeds. The job of separating the seeds from the stringy stuff is time-consuming, but it's amazing how children between the ages of seven and thirteen can get so much pleasure from doing this satisfying job.

Give them a baking tray to put the clean seeds onto and watch them get to it. Ask them to spread the seeds out evenly, and not more than two seeds deep. The seeds need to be sprinkled with a tablespoon of coarse salt, too.

When they're all washed, salted and ready, put the tray into the oven at whatever temperature it's set at for the main pumpkin dish, assuming it's a baked or roasted one. If not, set the oven to 180°C/350°F/Gas Mark 4. Put the tray of seeds in the hot oven and roast for about 20 minutes.

When they're cool, they need shelling before eating, which is a bit of a palaver, but enjoyable when you're little and you've made them yourself.

MAITAKE IN HONEY

Dried maitake mushrooms are a bit like shiitake, but even better for you. They are one of the most immune-system-boosting substances known to man. Independent scientific research from the US found that maitake mushrooms can have as strong a positive effect on people with HIV as the AZT drugs that most HIV patients are prescribed. In short, maitake are gentle yet powerful immune system boosters. They're particularly good for coughs and colds.

Maitake are generally considered a gourmet mushroom for grown ups, as kids can find the texture a bit strange. This is where disguise comes in. Simply mix a handful of dried maitake into a pot of manuka honey and leave to mingle for a few days. Manuka has a gentle antibiotic and healing effect due to the tea tree flowers that feed the bees who make it. Manuka and maitake is a great combination, full of healing potential and nice flavours. Spread it on toast soldiers, or mix it in hot water with a squeeze of lemon juice if you think your child's going down with a cold.

PS For another effective cold remedy, and one that may also help relieve asthma and other chesty problems, mix chopped raw onions and garlic, then soak them in honey and a little vinegar. Eat a teaspoon at a time, or spread on toast. It may sound revolting but it works!

KNICKERBOCKER GLORY

You're gonna need some long spoons and tall glasses for this one, but it'll keep them happy that they're getting a treat, and you happy that they're eating right.

Yogurt is great for adding more recruits to your kids' digestive flora, whatever milk it's cultured from. Flora are the little bugs inside the gut that keep your kids' general health and immunity up. Fresh & Wild stock yogurts from cow's milk of varying degrees of creaminess, plus lots of non-cow milk varieties. Try your kids on sheep's milk yogurt, goat's milk ones and non-dairy soy yogurts.

All are made to the same basic recipe – milk plus some bacterial culture. Coupled with a homemade fruit compote, it's a winning combination for health and deliciousness. If you're pushed for time, make an instant version using yogurt layered with organic ready-made fruit purées or fruit compote.

KNICKERBOCKER GLORY

FOR 4 LIP-SMACKIN' KNICKERBOCKER GLORIES:

2 Cox's apples
A handful of sultanas
A pinch of cinnamon
1 tablespoon corn malt syrup
450g live yogurt

Core the apples, then dice them. Put the apples, sultanas, cinnamon and a tablespoon of water into a small saucepan over a low heat. Put the lid on and leave to steam and stew for about 10 minutes. Give it a stir and see if there are still any chunks of apple that haven't gone mushy. If there are, replace the lid so the compote can cook some more. When it's done, remove the pan from the heat and stir in the syrup. Leave the compote to cool.

Get some tall glasses and fill with alternate layers of compote and yogurt, in about 2cm bands. Make the last layer yogurt. Serve with maple syrup in a squeezey sauce bottle, so the kids can draw little golden pictures onto the white yogurt.

SPELT MOUNTAINS

This recipe is very sweet, so it should only be served as a rare treat for occasions such as birthday parties. The good news is that the malt syrup doesn't break down as quickly as refined sugars, so the kids will get a lot less of a rollercoaster effect.

Spelt can be puffed a bit like puffed rice, and is sold in Fresh & Wild's breakfast cereals section. It comes ready-popped and coated with honey.

You can also make this recipe with amaranth, a tiny, white, round cereal grain native to South America. It's rich in lysine, protein, fibre and vitamins, and has a nutty taste and a sticky, gelatinous texture. Amaranth grains pop like popcorn, and are sold ready-popped and coated in honey in bags next to the puffed spelt. You can also find it at Fresh & Wild in the form of whole grains and flour for other lovely recipes.

1 tablespoon sunflower oil
200g puffed honeyed spelt
50g rolled oats
50g dried shredded coconut
75g chopped hazelnuts
100g butter
6 tablespoons barley malt syrup

Preheat the oven to 160°C/325°F/Gas Mark 3. Lightly oil a baking sheet with the oil. Mix the spelt, oats, coconut and hazelnuts in a big bowl. Melt the butter and syrup in a small pan, over a low heat, until they've melted just enough to become mixed and gooey. Pour this goo into the dry ingredients and mix everything together – it will be incredibly sticky.

Spoon dollops of the mixture onto the baking sheet, leaving a gap in between each one. Wait a few seconds until each dollop is cool enough to handle. Don't let the kids do the next bit just in case they misjudge the heat of the mixture. Before they get too cold and set, squeeze and shape them with your fingers to make craggy mountain shapes. Put them into the oven for about 20 minutes, until golden brown. Meanwhile, offer your child the bowl to lick as a thank you for helping. Leave the mountains on the tray to cool for a few minutes after they come out of the oven, then move them to make sure they don't stick to their spots. They'll be cool and ready to serve in about 15–20 minutes.

BEDTIME **AMAZAKE**

This one's easy to make, but takes a bit of time to deliver. It's great if you want to wean your child off their bedtime drink of cow's milk. They want the warming, reassuring comfort that a bottle of warm cow's milk can provide, but you're concerned about their asthma or eczema, too much catarrh or simply that they're having too much dairy.

If your kid is seriously into their milk, try diluting it with a little hot water mixed with a teaspoon of amazake. Slowly, over a few weeks, raise the proportion of diluted amazake to hot milk. Next, try mixing in a really top quality non-dairy milk, such as Bonsoy soy milk. The disguise is sadly unlikely to work with cheaper soy milk brands, although you might get away with homemade soy milk.

Amazake is made from fermented rice or millet and, as such, tastes malty. This fools your little one, as the lactose sweetness they like is replaced with a rich maltose sweetness they'll love. If you like malty bedtime drinks, try this to soothe yourself after a long day, too.

JUICES & SMOOTHIES

Gabriel David
Luscombe Organic Drinks, Buckfastleigh, Devon

'Using only the finest raw ingredients, our drinks are made by hand in small batches, combining the best traditional techniques and contemporary expertise. Each drink may vary slightly according to the rain and sun. But this is how seasonal hand-made drinks should be.'

J U I C E S

Why juice?

Because it's the quickest way to enjoy as many organic raw fruits and vegetables as you can fit in a glass.

Bursting with life, freshly made organic juices are a great idea for happy and healthy living.

The first stop is getting a decent juicer. There are two kinds, centrifugal and masticating. The centrifugal ones spin the mashed up fruit and veg at high speeds, so the juice flies out and is collected in a jug, while the pulp gets caught in a metal strainer. It's sort of like a liquidizer crossed with a high-powered salad spinner.

The masticating versions chew up the fruit and veg, breaking down the cell walls in the produce and therefore getting a lot more juice out of them. Not only is the pulp you throw away drier, but also the juice you get is more nutritious, as the liquid inside the cells is higher quality in terms of vitamins, minerals, enzymes, phytonutrients and flavour.

The drawbacks with masticators are price and time. Masticators cost more than centrifuges and take longer to extract the juice from your produce. So if you're new to juicing, it may be best to start with the cheaper centrifugal model (near enough any one will do, as they all have the same action) and then bite the bullet at a later stage – or drop some heavy hints come your birthday.

When you're ready to commit to seriously delicious and healthy treats, go for a Samson juicer. Not only can these babies do wheat grass (something it's not even worth attempting with a centrifugal), Samsons can do practically everything else except make a cup of tea. They can mince and chop any kind of food, from ginger to beef, and even mill flour from rice or any other grain. They can also extract sesame oil from raw or toasted sesame seeds, and make tahini and nut butters. They're one serious piece of culinary kit.

When it comes to juicing, the golden rule is ... make any combination of juices you fancy, but always stick to either all vegetable juices or all fruit juices. The exceptions to this rule are apple juice and carrot juice, which can be happily added to any kind of vegetable or fruit juice you like.

The cardinal juices that Fresh & Wild use are carrot, apple and orange, meaning that these three form the basis for all the juice mixtures sold in the stores. All the other juices added to these are in smaller amounts, because most other juices are generally pretty powerful in terms of flavour and their diuretic action. For example, drink too much celery juice and you might find yourself running to the loo. Beetroot juice, on the other hand, can act as a strong laxative.

Juicing should reflect the seasons as much as the rest of your recipes, if not more so. Using fruit and veg that's in season gives you the best tasting, most nutritious and most eco-friendly juices, in terms of the journey your produce has made. Seasonal juicing also has the advantage of being cost-effective. If something is locally grown and in season it usually means a lower price – and a better, fresher product.

Seasonal juicing means using fruit and veg at its juiciest and sweetest prime. New season carrots in early spring, for instance, have a much higher amount of liquid in them than tired old ones at the end of winter. Juice organic apples grown in England if at all available, and experiment with different varieties according to the season and your area.

Of course, the main reason lots of people juice is for their health. Here's a short list of reasons that people use different fruits and vegetables (but there are plenty more reasons to use each):

APPLES:

- contain malic acid, which removes impurities from the liver
- help your body to assimilate iron
- are highly alkaline and easily digestible

BEETROOT:

- dissolves acid crystals from the kidneys
- detoxifies the liver and gall bladder
- lubricates the intestines
- eliminates blood toxaemia, one of the causes of varicose veins
- is used by people with cancer as a part of Gerson therapy

BLUEBERRIES:

- are an excellent blood cleanser
- really do improve night vision
- protect the eyes from cataracts and glaucoma
- are natural laxatives

CARROTS:

- cleanse, nourish and stimulate almost every system in the body
- really are very good for the eyes and eyesight
- are great for the liver and intestinal tract
- lower blood cholesterol

CELERY:

- is a powerful diuretic
- contains silicon, which the body needs to repair ligaments and tendons
- purifies the blood
- contains coumarins, which help the activity of white blood cells
- tones the vascular system
- lowers blood pressure
- is useful to help treat and prevent migraines

FENNEL:

- relieves intestinal spasms and cramps
- tones and strengthens the stomach
- contains phytoestrogens, which help with periods and hot flushes

GINGER ROOT:

- helps blood circulation and therefore provides added energy
- quickly stops feeling of nausea
- helps digestion and the assimilation of the nutrients in food
- cleans the skin, bowels and kidneys from the inside

LEMONS AND LIMES:

- stimulate the liver and gall bladder
- have antiseptic properties
- are great for colds and sore throats

ORANGES:

- tone and purify the whole digestive system

- aid digestion because of their acid and sugar content
- contain lots of vitamin C

PARSLEY:
- is very high in vitamin C
- helps cleanse the blood of toxins
- keeps the blood vessels elastic, so helps prevent arteries hardening

SPINACH:
- is a laxative
- flushes toxic poisons out of the body
- repairs and maintains the colon for better colon health
- is good for the eyes, as it contains lots of vitamin A

STRAWBERRIES:
- are a fabulous skin cleansing food, whether juiced, eaten or applied
- contain ellagic acid, an anti-cancer compound
- are good for the intestines

In addition, any juice can have a booster added to it for even more targeted health-boosting properties. For example, add a shot of spirulina to a Colorado Detox juice for extra springtime detoxifying power, or echinacea tincture to a cup of Rise 'n' Shine Orange to help ward off a winter cold.

Fresh & Wild's tinctures are made from herbs mainly grown in Colorado by a man called Lorenzo Hayes. This area of the States is desert country, with sunshine 300 days of the year, but, being located in the foothills of the Rocky mountain range, it has a great supply of the purest mountain spring water and clean, clear mountain air. And there's a great deal of local herbal knowledge in this area too, right back to before the earliest foreign settlers and into pre-Columbus Native American history. These ideal geographical and cultural conditions, coupled with Lorenzo's fully-fledged flair, craft and dedication, results in the most beautiful herbs. Lorenzo and Linda Whitedove, a highly talented medical herbalist, then craft the herbs into potent herbal tinctures. And they understand the role of taste in good health, too.

Aromatherapists select **aromatherapy oils** in conjunction with the patient, who helps them choose **the right one** by indicating which oils they like the smell of.

Likewise, many naturopaths are beginning to believe that a herbal tincture that tastes good is much more likely to make the patient feel good. So the fact that Lorenzo and Linda artfully blend the tinctures with sweet-tasting spices, herbs and fruit extracts makes a lot of sense. They want their products to make you feel good and, ultimately, support your health.

Many herb companies grow and harvest their plants to a predetermined schedule. Lorenzo waits around until his plants are ready. He harvests the herbs at the best time for each of their growth cycles, instead of at the time that's most convenient for him. For instance, in the summer his echinacea flowers ripen one by one when they're ready. And he picks them just as they're ready, instead of averaging out the field and choosing one day for the whole lot (which would make his life a lot simpler). He knows that the quality of the flowers is better when they're all nice and ready. Likewise, he waits for three years before harvesting echinacea roots, finally pulling them up after the first frost of winter to make sure that the plant has focused its attention on its nether regions under the ground.

You can choose straight herbal tinctures like gingko or ginseng, or go for blends like echinacea – yes, Fresh & Wild's echinacea is actually a blend of two kinds of echinacea plants. A few other sensitively compiled mixtures that you may find useful are listed below, but there are plenty more to choose from in the stores:

Sleepyhead – something purely herbal that really does help you to get some sleep; made with fresh valerian root, passionflower vines, hops, skullcap, catnip and betony, plus lovely natural almond flavour.

Nervative – a natural herbal anti-depressant to make you feel sunny again; made with fresh St John's wort, oats, skullcap, catnip, Siberian ginseng, and motherwort, plus lemons.

Pure Woman – to generally support the female body and hormonal system in all its glory; made with chastetree berries, wild yam, Jamaican sarsaparilla, fresh hawthorn berries, oats, nettles, raspberry leaves, Siberian ginseng and damiana, plus strawberries.

Pure Man – to generally support the male body and hormonal system in all its glory; made with fresh saw palmetto berries, Siberian ginseng root, hawthorn berries, damiana, milk thistle seeds and oats, plus oranges.

Immunitive – an immunity-boosting concoction featuring some of our favourite Japanese mushrooms; made with astragalus, reishi, shiitake, maitake, and green tea.

Wheat grass juice is the major reason people usually take the plunge and treat themselves to a masticating juicer, as you can't extract juice from wheat grass in a centrifugal juicer. You can of course buy ready-made wheat grass juice blended with green tea, apple juice, agave syrup and spirulina – it's in the bottled drinks bit of the stores, and is made by Rabenhorst. You can also find freeze-dried wheat grass, barley grass and other detoxifying and energy-boosting greens in pots and jars in the natural remedies section of the stores. But freshly juiced wheat grass juice is seriously good for you. Just ask Christopher Maguire, the grain grass and living foods aficionado behind Fresh & Wild's trays of growing wheat and barley grasses and their optimum freeze-dried grass formula foods.

Christopher started juicing wheat and barley grasses in the 1970s, when the only store in the UK that sold them was Yehudi Menhin and Lillian Schofield's shop Whole Foods, in London's Baker Street. Christopher now runs a company called Rainbow Living Foods with his partner Sonia, and grows grass from at least 40 tons of grain every year. His own diet is made up of about 80 per cent raw vegan foods, hence he's full of beans, as anyone who's come across him will testify. But things weren't always this way ...

Christopher was a professional photographer. He learned about the power of raw foods and grain grass juice in the early 1970s from pioneer vegan nutritionists Viktoras Kulvinskas and Ann Wigmore, the promoters of the Hippocrates raw food diet. After becoming convinced this was the way ahead for him, Christopher wanted to drink wheat grass juice on a daily basis, but couldn't find a good enough supply to satisfy his own demand. So he started growing trays of it for himself, then his friends, then his friends' friends, and slowly but surely a whole chain of people grew by word of mouth, all wanting his amazing growing grains.

Time became more and more difficult to juggle, until Christopher finally had to decide which of his jobs to pursue – photography or living foods. Luckily for us, the living foods came up trumps, simply because so many of his customers were clamouring for them. This was the point that he moved the operation out of his big garden and onto a small farm in Sussex, calling this new business Green Seed.

Little did Christopher know that less than a decade later, he'd be moving to a 60-acre farm and forming the new business with Sonia. They continue supplying the very highest quality wheat and barley grasses, but have also added buckwheat and sunflower grasses to their range. All are grown from high quality, non-hybridized, heirloom grains indigenous to Northern Europe, because these are the grains that produce the best quality, most chlorophyll-rich, least allergenic, most mould-resistant grain grasses for health.

Grain grasses are incredibly concentrated, so most people who juice them have only 50–100ml per day. Serious fans like Christopher and Sonia drink up to 500ml per day, but that takes quite some juicing. Barley grass juices are milder in flavour than wheat grass juices, so might be a better bet for beginners. They're packed with natural enzymes as well as vitamins and minerals, so are a valuable addition to any adult diet or lifestyle.

If you're making juice of any kind for kids, it should be diluted with water so it's not too strong for them in terms of flavour, strength and sweetness. Fresh & Wild can dilute any of the juices with their Aquathin filtered water, which is also used to wash all their juicing equipment. This water goes through an Aquathin filtration system, which removes all the pollutants and minerals, so it is literally pure H_2O. You can also buy this water in the store from the Aquathin machine – and you can bring your own bottle to reuse it rather than throwing it away to go into landfill.

Each of the stores also sometimes has additional seasonal drinks unique to them. These sometimes get offered as a special if there's a glut of a particular vegetable or fruit. These have included Notting Hill's Hot Pear and Cinnamon Juice, Soho's Mango Smoothie, and Bristol's Blue Banana Smoothie. Catch them if you can.

The recipes I've listed below are for the entire range of regular classic Fresh & Wild juices, as sold in all the stores' juice bars. All of these juice recipes produce one 350ml glass, which is the equivalent of a large cup from a Fresh & Wild juice bar. As such, the recommended wheat grass

amount is a Fresh & Wild double shot. Juice the produce in the order listed, adding the cardinal juice last to take the finished mix up to the top of
the glass. Rinse your juice machine with water before making the next
juice, to keep the flavours as they should be, and always get rid of the
waste pulp between juices. Just feed these quantities of fresh produce
through a juicer to recreate the juicing staples that Fresh & Wilders enjoy ...

GREEN MACHINE
50ml wheatgrass
¼ a lemon, to taste
4–5 apples, to fill the glass

GRASSHOPPER
50ml wheatgrass
2–4cm piece ginger root, to taste
6–8 carrots, to fill the glass

WALDORF
2 sticks celery
¼ a lemon, to taste
2–4cm piece ginger root, to taste
4 apples, to fill the glass

COLORADO DETOX (OR CLIFTON DETOX IN THE BRISTOL STORE)
¼ medium beetroot or 1 small beetroot
2 sticks celery
¼ fennel
4–5 carrots, to fill the glass

RISE 'N' SHINE APPLE

3 apples

2–4cm piece ginger root, to taste

4 carrots, to fill the glass

RISE 'N' SHINE ORANGE

2 oranges

2–4cm piece ginger root, to taste

4 carrots, to fill the glass

VELVET UNDERGROUND

2 apples

½ medium beetroot, or 1 small beetroot

3 carrots, to fill the glass

POPEYE

2 sticks celery

A small handful spinach

A small bunch parsley

5–6 carrots, to fill the glass

SMOOTHIES

Smoothies are juices with either something creamy blended into them, or another thickening agent added, like mashed bananas.

Their **thick texture** makes most smoothies more like a **dessert than a drink**.

I also make **savoury smoothies** at home, using vegetable juices like carrot mixed with creamy yogurts, **psyllium husks** and dry-roasted **spices like cumin** – it's kind of like a savoury lassi, but thicker, creamier and **completely delicious**.

One of the very best Fresh & Wild smoothie thickeners is Cream o' Galloway frozen yogurt. The family behind this dairy delight are based out in the wilds of Scotland at Rainton Farm. The Finlay family have been farming their land since 1927, with successive generations passing down dairy secrets to the next. That's why Cream o' Galloway's frozen yogurt tastes so outrageously creamy and decadent and simply not at all low fat, even though it is. The frozen yogurts don't contain cream or eggs, and come in either plain or four lovely flavours – elderflower, honey and ginger, lemon meringue, and blackcurrant. Also, keep your eyes open for buffalo milk ice cream from Nick Griffin's buffalos in Milton Keynes, soon to be on the market.

Another great gloopy ingredient is mashed bananas. They're full of carbohydrates, both complex carbs and simple sugary ones. This means you get energy really quickly from them, but it lasts over a long period of time instead of giving you a quick sugar high and then a crash. They also contain the amino acid tryptophan, which helps you sleep and also helps the body develop sexual hormones. This doesn't mean that bananas necessarily make you horny, but they can certainly make you happy – especially as they're pretty low calorie, despite the general perception that they're a fattening food.

Bananas also contain a kind of fibre called pectin, which is the stuff that makes jams gel. Pectin helps the body detox, can also help heal any internal ulcers and it can lower blood cholesterol levels. Strangely, bananas are also excellent for sorting out both constipation and diarrhoea. And they've got loads of minerals and vitamins in them, including potassium, zinc, iron, folic acid, calcium and lots of the difficult-to-find vitamin B_6.

All of the following smoothie recipes make one 350ml glass, which is the equivalent of a large cup from a Fresh & Wild juice bar. If there are apples in the recipe, they need to be juiced in your juicer first, to make apple juice. If there are oranges listed in the recipe, they need squeezing with a citrus squeezer or citrus press. The apple or orange juices then need to be added to the creamy ingredients and whizzed in a *blender*, not a juicer. The creamy ingredients are the yogurts, strawberries, blueberries and bananas. Add the juice ingredient that's on the end of the ingredient list last, to make the drink up to the 350ml mark, and you'll have an authentic Fresh & Wild smoothie.

RED OM WITH ORANGE
1 banana
5–8 strawberries
60g Cream o' Galloway frozen yogurt, plain
2 oranges

RED OM WITH APPLE
1 banana
5–8 strawberries
60g plain creamy live yogurt
3 apples

MONKEY SHAKE (OR THE BANANA-RAMA IN BRISTOL)

60g fresh blueberries or ¼ punnet

1 banana

½ lemon to taste

3 oranges

PURPLE HAZE

60g blueberries

60g Cream o' Galloway frozen yogurt, plain

4 apples

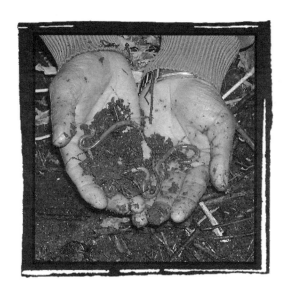

WHY ORGANIC?

'Healthy soil, healthy plants, healthy people.'

Eve Balfour, Founder of the Soil Association

For more information about organic food, visit my website: **Organicfood.co.uk**. Meanwhile, here are some of the health reasons that make me choose organic food whenever I can. The Big Four common sense reasons are:

ANTIBIOTICS, PESTICIDES, GM INGREDIENTS AND CHEMICAL FOOD ADDITIVES

Antibiotics are incredibly useful for treating illness. In fact, they've become an essential part of the treatment for many human diseases and medical procedures, from a toothache to open heart surgery. Nobody likes taking them, but most people do bite the bullet if their doctor tells them it's necessary.

Intensive animal farming is threatening to change all that. Because most non-organic farmers give their animals antibiotics routinely, antibiotics are losing their effectiveness for the human population. The reason farmers use them is to prevent diseases that would otherwise run rampant through the animals on their farms. The animals generally live too squashed together and in order to keep them in these cruel but cheap conditions, without them all keeling over, farmers dose them with antibiotics in increasingly high amounts.

Despite the humungous rise of organic food sales in the UK, non-organic animal farmers are on average giving their animals more drugs than ever – which is why you're bound to know someone who's taken a course of antibiotics that didn't work. Chances are that the bug they were trying to get rid of was wise to that drug, which means that if we're not careful, we could lose the magic of antibiotics in our medical kit.

Pesticides are poisons. That's the whole point. They are designed specifically to kill living things, pretty resilient living things actually – I'm talking about insects, the most successful class of living thing on the planet. Pesticides have to be strong and lethal, otherwise they wouldn't work. So it's not rocket science to discover that eating a whole bunch of different tiny amounts of pesticides all mixed together in your lunch might be a bad idea. If it's at all possible, I'd have thought it's a good idea to avoid them. And of course, it is completely possible simply by eating organically grown food.

GM ingredients are an experiment with our health and the global environment. I have no doubt that you're against genetic modification, because our pro-GM UK government's own nationwide survey of 2003, GM Nation, found that 98 per cent of Britons don't want it. And we're right. I can only assume that the other 2 per cent have a vested interest in a losing battle. GM will not feed the world, it will only trap farmers in developing countries in a vicious circle with the GM seed corporations.

GM seed can't be sown and reaped for its seed, like proper un-tampered seed. It has to be sown then bought and sown again the next year. That means that if the harvest fails one year and the farmer doesn't earn enough money for next year's seeds, he's stuffed.

The health claims of GM food are frankly unscientific, and what's worse, you simply can't recall these products once the pollen is out there. Every GM plant growing on the face of this planet pollutes the gene pool irrevocably. In short, GM sucks.

Chemical food additives vary wildly in their dubiousness, from traditional fairly-harmless-in-small-doses ones to new-fangled highly dodgy ones. They include artificial colourings like hyperactivity-promoting tartrazine; low-calorie sweeteners like the paradoxically appetite-stimulating Xylitol; flavour enhancers like MSG, which doesn't have to be listed on non-organic food; bone calcium leachers like the phosphoric acid in non-organic fizzy cola; and other processing chemicals that you're unlikely to want to eat. Organic food simply doesn't allow them.

When you eat really top organic ingredients, you'll find your weight will almost certainly become just right for your build. Your brain won't make you eat too much on its endless quest to find nutrition, as the balanced organic ingredients on your plate will give it a much better chance of finding the micro-nutrients it craves. The human brain detects the nutrition that it's getting and naturally makes you feel satisfied at the right time. Instead of getting bowled over by the deliciousness of the food in front of you, and ramming in one more portion than they should, people tend to find that they sit back after they've eaten enough and enjoy the feeling of satisfaction that a healthy organic meal delivers.

Of course, you need to be sensible about eating a varied diet, rich in veggies and fruit, and with pudding as a pudding and dinner as a dinner. But if you follow a basic level of common sense as to what's a staple food (fish, for instance) and what's an occasional treat (chocolate sauce), your weight will stabilize and you'll feel great.

If you eat an organic diet you'll find you eat just the right amount, fuelling your body with the energy you need for your full and busy life; it'll keep your neurotransmitters balanced for better stress-management, happiness and thinking power; and you'll provide your body with the vitamins, minerals, enzymes and phyto-chemicals to keep everything on track.

A decent bit of grub should balance all the elements – taste, texture, aroma and appearance. It should stimulate you and get your mouth watering simply by how it looks and smells. It's appetizing, aromatic, delicious to behold as well as taste. **Gimme real food – *bring it on.***

RESOURCES

ORGANIZATIONS

Fresh & Wild
www.freshandwild.com

Ysanne's website:
www.organicfood.co.uk

The Soil Association	www.soilassociation.org
Pesticide Action Network UK	www.pan-uk.org
Natural Discovery	www.naturaldiscovery.co.uk
Bristol Cancer Help Centre	www.bristolcancerhelp.org

SOURCES

The Little Food Book by Craig Sams
Published by Alastair Sawday Publishing, 2003
www.littleearth.co.uk/food

Superfoods by Michael van Straten and Barbara Griggs
Published by Dorling Kindersley, 1990
www.michaelvanstraten.com

Good Fish Guide by Bernadette Clarke
Published by Marine Conservation Society, 2002
www.mcsuk.org

In Too Deep – The Welfare of Intensively Farmed Fish by Philip Lymbery
Published by Compassion in World Farming Trust, 2002
www.ciwf.co.uk

The Bakers of Paris and the Bread Question, 1700–1775 by Steven Kaplan
Published by Duke University Press, 1996
www.dukeupress.edu

All About Cookery by Mrs Isabella Beeton
Vintage 1920s' book from 'the finest housekeeper in the world'
Published by Ward Lock & Co.

RECOMMENDED READING

More books by Ysanne:

Farmers' Market Round-the-Seasons Cookbook by Ysanne Spevack
Published by Southwater Publishing, 2004

The Organic Kitchen by Ysanne Spevack
Published by Lorenz Books, 2004

Organic Kitchen and Garden by Ysanne Spevack, Christine Lavelle and
Michael Lavelle
Published by Anness Publishing, 2004

The Real Taste of Japan by Ysanne Spevack, John Bellame and Jan Bellame
Published by Cross Media, 2004

Organic Cookbook by Ysanne Spevack
Published by Lorenz Books, 2002

Branding Healthy Foods: Organic, Functional and Whole Foods by Ysanne
Spevack
Published by Reuters Business Insight, 2001

Cookbooks by other authors:

Madhur Jaffrey's Ultimate Curry Bible by Madhur Jaffrey
Published by Random House, 2003

Eat Smart, Eat Raw by Kate Wood
Published by Grub Street, 2002

The Boxing Clever Cookbook by Jacqui Jones and Joan Wilmot
Published by J & J Publishing, 2002

Indian Market Cookbook: Recipes from Santa Fe's Coyote Cafe by Mark Millar
Published by Ten Speed Press, 1995

Tamarind and Saffron by Claudia Roden
Published by Penguin, 1999

Cranks' Fast Food by Nadine Abensur
Published by Cassell & Co, 2000

Paradiso Seasons by Denis Cotter
Published by Atrium, 2003

Real Chocolate by Chantal Coady
Published by Quadrille, 2003

Organic Superfoods by Michael van Straten
Published by Mitchell Beazley, 1999

The Cinnamon Club Cookbook by Iqbal Wahhab and Vivek Singh
Published by Absolute Press, 2003

Taste: A New Way to Cook by Sybil Kapoor
Published by Mitchell Beazley, 2003

Food for thought:

Not on the Label by Felicity Lawrence
Published by Penguin, 2004

Fast Food Nation by Eric Schlosser
Published by Allen Lane / Penguin Press, 2001

Take It Personally by Anita Roddick
Published by Thorsons, 2001

Gardening for the Future of the Earth by Howard Yana-Shapiro and John
    Harrisson
Published by Bantam Books, 2000

The Optimum Nutrition Bible by Patrick Holford
Published by Piatkus, 1997

The Grocers: The Rise and Rise of the Supermarket Chains by Andrew
     Seth and Geoffrey Randall
Published by Kogan Page, 1999

No Logo by Naomi Klein
Published by Flamingo / HarperCollins 2000

Living with Chickens by Jay Rossier
Published by The Lyons Press, 2002

The Great Food Gamble by John Humphrys
Published by Coronet, 2002

Whole Foods Companion by Diane Onstad
Published by Chelsea Green, 1996

Rick Stein's Guide to the Food Heroes of Britain by Rick Stein
Published by BBC Consumer Publishing, 2003

WITH THANKS TO ...

Steve Cook, for being so fab while I was tap tap tapping this book, and Jacqueline Bellefontaine, for being such a talented home economist, and all the other people who've added kindnesses (with their culinary preferences or specialities):

Adele Nozedar (basil), Alex Parks (water), Alex Poots (fine finger foods), Alice Waters at Chez Panisse (slowly does it), Alison Wright (apple pie), Annalisa and Gabriella Blake (chocolate mousse cake), Antony Worrall Thompson (beef), Barbara Rayner and Helen Browning Organics (organic veal), Bernard Fanning (bourbon), Bob and Carolyn Kennard at Graig Farm (roast leg of mutton), Brett Anderson and Santucia (throat coat tea), Carl and Diana Ryden (Swedish seafood), Caroline Woffenden at Marine Stewardship Council (shellfish), Craig Sams at the Soil Association (macrobiotics and jelly), Cyrus Todiwala, MBE, at Café Spice Namasté (eggs), Dad (yet to find the mystery room), Danny and Mark at Third Space (exercise), Dave Lee (dried mushrooms), Dido Fisher (avocados), Dorothy Woodend (chocolate), Ed Chocolate (real bacon butties), Elizabeth Winkler (anything organic), Fuschia Dunlop (Szechuan), Glenn Max (chocolate), Grant Morrison and Kristen (chocolate), Glenn Skinner (proper puff pastry), Guy LaFayette (hemp seeds), Gyrus (mock bacon butties), Howard and Nancy Yana-Shapiro at Seeds of Change (exquisite salads), James Little at Natural Discovery (seaside specials), Janet and Ross Anderson from East Lochhead Farm (heirloom beasts), Jane Dick at Fundamentally Fungus (fresh mushrooms), Jill Pliskin (perfect coffee), Jim Manson (wholefoods), Jo Hodder at the Society of Authors (champagne), Jo Mcallister and Alex Brattel (real food), John Barrow at the Organic Delivery Company (his wife's), Johnny Dee (pasta), Kate Pengelly at Pesticide Action Network UK (avocados), Kate Sebag at Tropical Wholefoods (exotic fruits), Kate Wood (raw everything), Kirsty Hawkshaw (apples), Leigh Ferguson (raw juices), Leigh Morrison and Craig Robertson (chocolate), Lindsay Finelli and family (the original cake baker), Lotte at Southern Alps (strawberry strawberry), Louise Edge and Belinda Fletcher at Greenpeace (sustainably packaged), Marie-Louise Flexen (tiki cocktails), Marion Deuchars (rooibosch chai), Mark Miller at Coyote Café (tamales), Mark Steene at Seasoned Pioneers (spicy),

Martin Christy at Seventypercent.com (70% or above), Melanie Dkik and family (Persian chicken), Michael Bateman (fine wines), Michael van Straten (spicy kumquats), Momo at Sketch (beautifully cooked), Moyra Bremner (ethical), Mum (everything with flair), Nick the Record (genmai), Nikki Smith (fresh), Peter Hayes (marzipan chocolate), Peter Grosvenor at Jefferson's Seafoods (a good bit of Cornish fish), Peter Scholey (real ale), Peter Sellars (hand-crafted and authentic), Peter Sissons (gourmet vegetarian), Richard Ehrlich (fine dining), Roanne Bell (Japanese noodles), Roopa Gulati (North Indian/Cumbrian fusion), Russell Hobbs (Breadman bread), Sarah Beattie (South American), Sarah Ratty at Ciel (roast veggies), Saul Galpern (coffee), Steve Chandra Savale (Gaby's), Sherman and Phil Bennett (steak), Susan Cook (Mexican), Sweety Kapoor (Mumbai home cooking), Tracie Evans (cake), Vanessa Sanders (Yorkshire puds), Vikki Liogier, Dave Hine and Alex (puy lentils)

And with thanks to all those who helped this book happen at ...

Fresh & Wild:

Peter Bradford, Bryan and Tara Meehan, Margreet Westerhuis, Jeff Rotheram, Adam Lord, Riccardo Sainz, Katie Cordle, Maz Hurley, Diana Cooper, Aylie Cooke, Andy Evans, Mark Woollard, Tamlyn Martins, Andy Payne

HarperCollins:

Wanda Whiteley, Belinda Budge, Susanna Abbott, Sarah Stewart, Becky Glibbery, Jacqui Caulton, Simon Gerratt, Kathy Dyke, Jillian Stewart, James Cowen, Ben North, Chris Wold, Chiara Priorelli

INDEX

S P E C I A L   O F F E R

Order these selected Thorsons and Element titles direct from the publisher and receive £1 off each title! Visit www.thorsonselement.com for additional special offers.

Free post and packaging for UK delivery (overseas and Ireland, £2.00 per book).

The Bodydoctor David Marshall (ISBN 0-00-717685-6)	£14.99 - £1 = £13.99
Only Fat People Skip Breakfast Lee Janogly (ISBN 0-00-717699-6)	£7.99 - £1 = £6.99
Life DIY Pete Cohen (ISBN 0-00-717280-X)	£9.99 - £1 = £8.99
Cooking Without Barbara Cousins (ISBN 0-72254022-1)	£10.99 - £1 = £9.99

Place your order by post, phone, fax, or email, listed below. Be certain to quote reference code **713L** to take advantage of this special offer.

Mail Order Dept. (REF: **713L**)
HarperCollins*Publishers*
Westerhill Road
Bishopbriggs G64 2QT

Email: customerservices@harpercollins.co.uk
Phone: 0870 787 1724
Fax: 0870 787 1725

Credit cards and cheques are accepted. Do not send cash. Prices shown above were correct at time of press. Prices and availability are subject to change without notice.

BLOCK CAPITALS PLEASE

Name of cardholder _____

Address of cardholder _____
_____
_____

Postcode _____

Delivery address (if different)
_____
_____
_____

Postcode _____

I've enclosed a cheque for £_____, made payable to HarperCollins*Publishers*, or please charge my Visa/MasterCard/Switch (circle as appropriate)

Card Number: _____
Expires: __/__   Issue No: __/__   Start Date: __/__
Switch cards need an issue number or start date validation.

thorsons
element

Signature:_____